Breath from Heaven

God's Presence in the Face of a Pandemic

Phyllis Benigas

Paperback ISBN: 978-1-64719-010-1
Epub ISBN: 978-1-64719-011-8
Mobi ISBN: 978-1-64719-012-5

Published by BookLocker.com, Inc., St. Petersburg, Florida.

Unless otherwise indicated, all Scripture quotations are taken from the *Holy Bible*, New Living Translation, copyright © 1996, 2004, 2015 by Tyndale House Foundation. Used by permission of Tyndale House Publishers, Inc., Carol Stream, Illinois 60188. All rights reserved.

Scripture quotations marked MSG are taken from *THE MESSAGE*, copyright © 1993, 2002, 2018 by Eugene H. Peterson. Used by permission of NavPress. All rights reserved. Represented by Tyndale House Publishers, Inc.

Scripture quotations marked NIV are from the Holy Bible, New International Version®, NIV® Copyright © 1973, 1978, 1984, 2011 by Biblica, Inc.® Used by permission. All rights reserved worldwide.

Scripture quotations marked KJV are from the King James Version of the Bible.

Library of Congress Cataloging in Publication Data
Benigas, Phyllis
Breath from Heaven: God's Presence in the Face of a Pandemic by Phyllis Benigas
Library of Congress Control Number: 2020918189

Printed on acid-free paper.

BookLocker.com, Inc.
2020

To Tom, the love of my life, who
gathered an army of believers to pray for my
healing. God heard and answered their prayers!

ACKNOWLEDGMENTS

My Deep Appreciation To:

My family! They never gave up on me, never gave in to negative reports, and believed every moment for my complete healing. They supported me with encouragement and prayers throughout the writing of this story during recovery. My forever love and thanksgiving to my beloved Tom, Mandy and Bryan, Giana, Jett, Brady and Lacey, Kai, Karis, Brenda and Cliff, Jon and Susan, Melody and Rod, Allyson and Matt, Reed and Britta, Lori, and many cousins.

Believers around the world who prayed for my healing from hospitalization to recovery, making this writing of God's faithfulness a possibility.

My dear college friend, Judy McEachran, who blessed me with her gifted, anointed piano ministry while I was recovering and writing. Her music is available on youtube.com/Judy McEachran. You'll be blessed!

The Europe Region Missions family led by Paul and Angie Trementozzi, their call to prayer on my behalf, and personal support. Our Western Europe team, Mark and Dalene Good, Dalene's anointed counsel during my recovery. And our CTS colleagues who prayed and supported me in so many ways.

Angela Hoy and the great team at BookLocker, committed to making authors' dreams come true!

TABLE OF CONTENTS

FOREWORD

I have had the joy of knowing Phyllis for about two decades. Whether ministering to youth across Florida, arranging missionary visits, serving on the Assemblies of God World Missions Board, or working as a missionary in Europe, her heart for ministry and missions is clear. She demonstrates God's love in word and deed to His people and those outside the circle of God's amazing grace.

This book relating her experience with COVID-19 is filled with the grace of God. I can closely identify with her journey. After my COVID-19 diagnosis this spring, I was in a medically induced coma and intubated for 34 days, then isolated for the next 26 days. I survived dialysis, various infections (including sepsis), blood clots, double viral pneumonia, and ARDS (acute respiratory distress syndrome). I recently completed inpatient and outpatient rehab and can testify to God's miraculous healing power.

You will be encouraged by the way Phyllis's story demonstrates the love of God, the power of His Word, and the importance of family in surviving a health crisis. In her struggle with COVID-19, Phyllis lived out the teaching of her godly mother: "You can't look at circumstances. You have to keep your eyes on Jesus." What great advice. Our lives are like roller coaster rides, packed with highs and lows. Wherever you find yourself now—high or low—you will be encouraged by Phyllis's reminder to lift your eyes to Jesus.

May the Lord strengthen you with His Word, no matter what you're facing.

— Greg Mundis, D.Min.
Executive Director
Assemblies of God World Missions

INTRODUCTION

Pandemic. Coronavirus. It happened so fast. I read about its potential through the media, just as I had learned about past infectious diseases. I didn't expect it to impact my personal world. But it did.

I received the diagnosis of coronavirus infection on March 20, 2020, and was immediately hospitalized. The doctor informed me that my condition was grave, and her best option was to connect the ventilator. We would wait and see. I was unable to say goodbye to my husband, Tom, at the time but received this text from him later, minutes before the ventilator was connected: "You won't believe the number of people praying for you…receive the peace of God. 'Peace I leave with you; my peace I give you. I do not give to you as the world gives. Do not let your heart be troubled and do not be afraid.' (John 14:27, NIV) Everyone is praying!" I was so sick that it was difficult to respond, but I finally managed, "The struggle to breathe is more exhausting than I can describe. A couple of times, I've been tempted just to stop. Constantly receiving bad news. May all these prayers be answered today." Tom's quick response was, "Don't quit! There are so many people praying for you." With no strength left to text the names of my precious family and close friends, I merely texted, "I love everyone." And with that, the doctor connected me to the ventilator for six days.

How do we get through weeks of hospitalization and months at home recovering from illness? How do we get through *any* severe ailment, terrible loss, or heartbreak? I can testify that the most significant help comes from our Creator, the one who knows us and loves us the most. The Lord was with me every step of the way, every isolated moment, and He provided everything I needed to make it through even the most challenging days ahead of me.

No matter what you are facing today, our loving God will provide just what you need to give you hope and peace and see you through to victory no matter what your struggle. The following pages reveal God's hand at work in the darkest hour of my life. Perhaps in your reading, you will gain new insights or be reminded of what you can do to move from doubt and fear in your crisis to hope and trust in the Lord.

I hope your life right now is free from challenges. If so, how wonderful! However, I know you have a relative or friend who is desperate for help at this moment. Through reading this story, I pray *you* are the catalyst to help them discover the answer, the Lord, their Shepherd, who will guide them through to the other side of their trial.

As days turned to weeks in the hospital, I found myself astounded by God's help and presence in my isolated room. I knew He was calling me to pay attention and remember all that was happening, not so much about my physical condition, but instead about the help and tools He gave me that brought peace and hope. I also knew He was calling me to write and share my story with you. In obedience to Him like David of old, I am sharing my account of His *righteous ways,* "I'll write the book on your righteousness, talk up your salvation the livelong day, never run out of good things to write or say...You got me when I was an unformed youth, God, and taught me everything I know. *Now I'm telling the world your wonders; I'll keep at it until I'm old and gray...*[I'll] get out the news of your strong right arm to this world, news of your power to the world yet to come, Your famous and righteous ways, O God. God, you've done it all! Who is quite like you?" (Psalm 71:14-19, MSG, emphasis added)

Chapter 1

PANDEMIC

"I was facing death, and he saved me. Let my soul be at rest again, for the Lord has been good to me."
(Psalm 116:5-7)

Pandemic. Coronavirus. It happened so fast. I read about its potential through the media, just as I had learned about past infectious diseases. I didn't expect it to impact my personal world. I never left home without my little bottle of hand sanitizer and already possessed a healthy space bubble as part of my behavior. I cautiously moved forward with this new threat in our world.

My husband Tom and I are missionaries to Europe, based in Brussels, Belgium. On weekends, we travel throughout the continent of Europe, ministering and assisting in international churches. We love it! We enjoy the multicultural connection in these churches and the delightful traditional worship that each culture brings as we worship together. During the week, we serve at Continental Theological Seminary (CTS), where Tom is the campus pastor, giving us the opportunity to mentor and encourage students from over 30 countries who are training for ministry. What a joy!

Suddenly our world, busy but always fulfilling, was altered just like the rest of the world. We canceled the daily chapel services we directed at CTS, classes went online, and church doors were closed. Many decisions were made the week of March 8, 2020, as governments in Europe began to stop travel, shut down businesses and schools, and confine their citizens to home.

Our weekend ministry in Malmo, Sweden, was canceled for March 13-15. On Saturday, March 14, I started to run a low-grade fever, felt achy, and fatigued. The following Tuesday, I called my General Practitioner, and he informed me that the hospital would take me when I developed breathing problems in addition to the other symptoms. On Friday, I called him once again and reported breathing problems, no appetite, and fatigue. He told me to go directly to the hospital for an examination. And so, the journey began.

Tom and I arrived at the hospital and went to the check-in desk. The receptionist instructed me to sit in the waiting room until she called my name and told Tom to leave the hospital the way he came in. I had no idea I would be admitted that day and brought nothing with me in preparation for it. I handed Tom my wallet and kept only my Belgian ID card, phone, and small purse. Little did I know that this was the last time I would see Tom for 21 days. Upon examination, I was admitted to the Covid19 ICU area, immediately put on oxygen, administered a nasal coronavirus swab test, and a CT Scan of my lungs. The doctor did not inform me of the results of the scan at the time, but later I learned my lungs were 25% and 10% infected.

My hospital experience to date was the delivery of two babies, but suddenly my world became one of IV's, blood tests, and nurses covered from head to toe with protective gear. The nurses brought food, but I had no appetite and couldn't eat. To keep my strength, I received nutrition through an IV, along with several other liquids. My prayer during these first few hours was for God to heal me and comfort Tom and my family. I have no idea what my *prayer language* was communicating to the Lord, but I knew He was listening.

On Tuesday, March 24, another CT Scan was taken of my lungs, and shortly afterward, a doctor came to see me. She looked me in the eyes, told me that the virus had gotten worse and that my condition was very grave. My lungs were 75% infected with the virus. When first admitted to the hospital, I was hesitant to allow the use of hydroxychloroquine because of heart issues in my family history. When the doctor asked once again to use this medicine, I said yes, yes, whatever it takes. She felt the only recourse was to put me on the ventilator. I asked her to call my husband and let him know, and she said she most definitely would do it.

On March 24, I was connected to a ventilator. I didn't know what this device entailed precisely or if it would last for a day or a week. Later in recovery, I was told that I was the first coronavirus patient put on the ventilator at this hospital. The doctor wondered if the anesthetic was sufficient and asked if I remembered any of it. And remember, I did. At that moment speaking with her, I recalled more than I desired, especially the initial connection.

It was absolutely the most frightening moment of my life, and all I could think was *what have I done, God save me!* I drifted in and out of awareness and lost all concept of time over the next six days. However, Tom was very conscious of time, every minute of it. He later told me he drove to the hospital every day while I was on the ventilator and sat in the parking lot so that he could be near me and pray. I don't think I need to express how much this means to me. We have a great love for each other, and I am blessed beyond measure.

During those days, Tom contacted all our family members and kept them up to date. Through Facebook, he gathered an army of believers from all over the world, asking them to pray for me. He posted almost daily, reporting and soliciting prayer. Our friends, people I had never met, prayer groups, churches, and missionaries prayed daily for me, and I believe that is why I am alive today. I know that God guided the doctors in the wise decisions they made concerning me. One doctor told me that I was the talk of the medical community at that point because I was one of the first in my age group to recover after the ventilator. It was early in the pandemic.

At one point, towards the end of my time on the ventilator, I remembered a doctor saying that the device had done its job. Someone approached me with what I thought was maybe a toothbrush with a strong-tasting substance on it and started to touch my lips and teeth. I didn't understand what was happening, and the substance began to choke me. I tried to push away the individual, and then before I knew it, I was slipping once again into that frightening world of the ventilator. The doctor called

Tom and told him they tried to remove the ventilator, but I became agitated and was reconnected.

Receiving this information was one of the most challenging moments for Tom during my illness. A few years earlier, his cousin was connected to a ventilator after heart surgery and became agitated when the doctors tried to remove it. He eventually died connected to it. Imagine the thoughts that flooded Tom's mind as the doctor spoke with him. He testifies that because of the many prayers on our behalf, he had the strength to refuse those negative thoughts and claimed victory for me. The next day the ventilator was successfully removed, and I was moved to ICU for recovery.

Don't stop reading here! As my story continues, God's faithfulness is revealed at every turn. It demonstrates the behaviors we can make a part of each day to carry us along while walking through life's challenges. As you read, you will see how the Lord guided my thought life and brought stability to my emotions. The response we give when facing a crisis is crucial to our victory, and I pray that the following chapters provide encouragement and guidance for any challenge you may face. My heart declares with David, "I've thrown myself headlong into your arms—I'm celebrating your rescue. *I'm singing at the top of my lungs*, I'm so full of answered prayers." (Psalm 13:5-6, MSG, emphasis added)

You are never alone. God is with you. And He will help you!

Chapter 2

HIDDEN WORDS

"I have hidden your word in my heart, that I might not sin against you." (Psalm 119:11)

A Beam of Light

With the ventilator removed on the sixth day, my consciousness returned. I was extremely weak in body, yet my mind was very active. How do you pass the time in isolation, lying in bed for days on end? How do you control your thought process when faced with uncertainty and so many questions? I was sure of only one solution, and that was to ask God to help me.

From the first day of consciousness, the Lord was with me, answering my heart's cry for help. Suddenly, Bible verses started to flood my thinking, each one bringing a peace and joy all its own. He brought back to my remembrance the dozens of verses I had committed to memory, even those I learned at my mother's insistence when I was young. To inspire me to memorize, mom often quoted, "Thy Word is a lamp unto my feet, and a light unto my path." (Psalm 119:105, KJV) Back in those days, the King James Version was her only option, and I love those familiar words. Today, I am equally blessed by other Bible versions, including *The Message* version of this passage, which says, "By your words I can see where I'm going; they throw *a beam of light* on my dark path." (Emphasis added) Another favorite verse of moms was, "Thy Word have I hid in my heart that I might not sin against thee." (Psalm 119:11, KJV) She made sure I memorized at least one verse every week.

There were many other activities I would have preferred doing as a child other than devoting part of my Saturday to scripture memorization. However, at this moment in time—isolated in my hospital room with only occasional visits by nurses covered in yellow protective gear, surrounded by daunting medical equipment, IV therapy, oxygen therapy, and more tubes attached to me than I care to describe—those scriptures were the priceless *beam of light*, *hidden* in my heart, to guide me forward.

My church reinforced the scripture memorization protocol I received at home. When I could barely read, my Children's Church teacher offered a special prize to anyone who would memorize an *entire chapter* in the Bible and quote it within the next couple of Sundays. I had memorized all the regular scripture verses that children tend to know at this point, but this task seemed impossible for me until I chanced upon Psalm 117. It was short and sweet, and with my mom's help, I memorized it!

There were two or three of us who took the easy route and quoted Psalm 117, and we still received the prize, which was a miniature copy of the Book of John.

That teacher was going to get the Word of God into us one way or another! This easy strategy wasn't a bad idea considering the truth it delivered to my young soul.

Psalm 117 declares, "Praise the Lord, all you nations. Praise him, all you people of the earth. For he loves us with unfailing love; the Lord's faithfulness endures forever. Praise the Lord!" Psalm 117 is the shortest chapter in the Bible as well as the center chapter of the Bible. It may be short, but it declares two unchangeable characteristics of God: *God's love for us will never fail, and His faithfulness to us will last forever.* Furthermore, this love and faithfulness are not just for Israel, but *all nations*, Jews and Gentiles alike—Psalm 117 encourages the whole world to praise the Lord!

My theology at that young age in Children's Church was not much further along than God is Love, but I knew, to a measure, what love was and who God was. The fact that His love for me would never fail has stayed with me my entire life and has carried me through many discouraging moments, including the one I was facing. In that isolated hospital room, the truths of Psalm 117 undergirded me—God's love never fails, and His faithfulness never ends, regardless of my present circumstance.

Even though we grow more sophisticated in our theology as we age and hopefully more intimate in our relationship with God, the *foundation* never changes—God's love and faithfulness will last forever, and His love is for everyone. This message can touch the youngest of hearts, and I know they understand it just as

I did. We limit the impact God's Word can make in a child's life when we assume they would not understand.

The scriptures we memorize early in life become a part of our spiritual DNA, something to draw on throughout life. God's word hidden in our hearts is an unseen source that influences our response to everything we experience. Christian Neuroscientist Dr. Caroline Leaf explains it this way, "When we implant God's word into our minds, we fill our brains with the powerful environmental influence of God's love, which directly impacts mental and physical health in a positive direction."[1]

I remember the first time I read the account in Deuteronomy 6 of Moses instructing the Israelites on the importance and impact of God's commandments. "Love God, your God, with your whole heart: love him with all that's in you, love him with all you've got! *Write these commandments that I've given you today on your hearts. Get them inside of you and then get them inside your children.* Talk about them wherever you are, sitting at home or walking in the street; talk about them from the time you get up in the morning to when you fall into bed at night. Tie them on your hands and foreheads as a reminder; inscribe them on the doorposts of your homes and on your city gates." (Deuteronomy 6:5-9, MSG, emphasis added)

Clearly, God's holy words were taken seriously by the Israelites. Sometime later in Israel's history, orthodox Jews carried out these scriptures literally. They copied verses, placed them in a small box called a frontlet, and wore them on their foreheads. They nailed copied scriptures on the doorposts of their homes. Many still do this today during prayer.

We didn't practice these instructions by Moses in my home, but scripture verses were a part of everyday life, starting at breakfast. On the kitchen table sat a little box in the shape of a loaf of bread, and it held small cards displaying a scripture verse on each side. I understood that mom expected me to choose a card from *The Bread of Life* promise box every morning and read it to her. Her response each time was, "Oh, that's such a good one!" I remember thinking at times that it would be simply *impossible* to pick a bad one. Many times, the card was chosen while shoving down toast or cereal in a hurry to leave for school, but the exercise served its purpose. The Creator of the universe spoke a promise to me that I could draw from any time of the day. I learned early in life just how powerful His Word is to touch lives in a personal sense each day, just as it was doing now in my hospital bed.

His Word is Alive and Powerful

A former missionary to China attended my home church when I was a child. Doris was forced to leave China in the early 1950s when the Communist regime came into power. To abandon the Chinese people was a dreadful moment in her life, and she often cried and asked our congregation to remember the Christians left behind. She asked us to pray that God would protect them and that they would be a light in a very dark place.

Doris' only consolation was that over the span of her years in China, she and other missionaries had emphasized scripture memorization. Doris rejoiced over the scriptures hidden in the hearts of Chinese believers when Bibles were ripped out of their hands and destroyed. Reports today out of China reveal that the Church is alive and well and growing in that nation regardless of the suppressive government. This is possible because God's Word hidden in the hearts of believers is *alive* and carries an agenda all its own. "For the word of God is alive and powerful." (Hebrews 4:12a)

God's Word is personal, up to the moment, *measuring the thoughts and desires* of everyone. When these dedicated missionaries could no longer guide and teach, they believed that the memorized scripture fulfilled its destiny in the heart of each believer. "It is sharper than the sharpest two-edged sword, cutting between soul and spirit, between joint and marrow. It exposes our innermost thoughts and desires. Nothing in all creation is hidden from God." (Hebrews 4:12b,) In answer to Doris' prayer and the prayers of countless others, believers in China matured in their faith and kept that faith under the watchful eye of God's Word. Although the church went underground and persecution continued, the Church has flourished in China under communism. Christianity is the fastest-growing religion in China, and many believe there to be well over 100 million believers today.

Through the centuries, from the early Church to today, many people groups have experienced similar persecution. We read stories of how God's Word was recorded long ago, hand-copied, memorized and passed along in communities, every word more precious than gold. This history passed from generation to generation should say something to us.

These accounts, along with my own hospital experience, confirm the value of His Word committed to memory. Currently, it's difficult to imagine not having a Bible at our fingertips, whether in print or online. But, yes, it happened to me in the hospital when I needed it most. We have no idea what the future holds for us.

The Comfort and Conviction of His Word

Through the years, I recalled scriptures from memory on countless occasions while encouraging a hurting soul, as Paul said in I Thessalonians 5:11, "Encourage one another and build each other up." (NIV) Words cannot express the blessing my daughter Mandy has been to me in this area. After I was released from the hospital and sent home to recover, her daily phone calls from the United States gave me the encouragement I so desperately needed. Straight from her heart and her time in prayer, she quoted scripture after scripture about the goodness of God. She quoted scriptures filled with the promises of God, and I would weep. Mandy, too, had memorized a vast number of Bible verses through the years, and they flowed spontaneously as she ministered to me. They brought life and hope as I struggled with complications from the virus, and I will always remember her spirit-led ministry as she *encouraged and built me up.*

Memorized scripture verses help us share the good news. "Always be prepared to give an answer to everyone who asks you to give the reason for the hope that you have." (I Peter 3:15, NIV) We often feel inadequate or hesitant to share the *good news* with others, questioning our ability to express it or the acceptance of our message. However, I think we forget that when we *give the reason for the hope we have* in Christ, we link arms with the world's greatest evangelist, the Holy Spirit, whose anointing graces both God's Word and our message. This anointing is irresistible to those who are seeking answers.

We are adequate *and* have everything we need for our witness because "[The Holy Spirit] will teach you everything and will remind you of everything I have told you." (John 14:26) The acceptance of our message is not our responsibility, but that of the Holy Spirit, "[The Holy Spirit] will convict the world of its sin, and of God's righteousness, and of the coming judgment." (John 16:8) The Holy Spirit brings to our remembrance God's Word, we share its message, and the Holy Spirit does His job to convict. What a team!

Whether to bring comfort to a hurting soul or answers to someone seeking a Savior, His Word is what we need. What a joy it is when God's Word seamlessly flows from my memory, without hesitation, with no risk of losing the best moment to touch someone's life with that living Word from Heaven.

Now, while lying in my hospital bed, I, too, was touched by this *hidden* Word. Its continual encouragement prompted me to pray more than once that

I would again have the opportunity to share its wealth with others. I believed that God would raise me to do just that.

His Word is Supernatural—Always Hits Its Target!

"As the rain and the snow come down from heaven, and do not return to it without watering the earth and making it bud and flourish, so that it yields seed for the sower and bread for the eater, so is my word that goes out from my mouth: It will not return to me empty, but will accomplish what I desire and achieve the purpose for which I sent it." (Isaiah 55:10-11, NIV) God's Word is supernatural, and it always hits its target!

I've heard many stories about the tenacity of God's Word to touch lives when sent out to accomplish its purpose, and one such account comes to mind. I don't remember all the details surrounding the story, but the *destiny* of a single Bible verse remains forever in my memory. A man in his fifties was going through a difficult situation. He was not a church attender and did not profess a religious belief but found himself remembering a scripture verse he had heard as a child of seven or eight when he attended Sunday School the first and only time in his life.

Desperate for help and unable to get past this verse, the man visited a church in his area and asked the pastor to explain what the verse meant. That day changed everything for Him! The pastor shared with him about the love of God and led this seeker to the Lord. What a great example of Isaiah's words, "So is my word that goes out from my mouth: It will not return to me empty, but will accomplish what I desire and achieve the purpose for which I sent it." Over 40 years later, a verse heard in Sunday School as a young boy changed a man's eternal destiny.

It cannot fail! Success guaranteed! I can testify that the living Word hit the target and achieved its purpose of filling me with hope and faith when I needed it most in my hospital bed. The scripture verses *hidden in my heart* brought hours of comfort and helped pass the many days in isolation as I recalled their truths. When we call on God to help us, He has an unlimited number of solutions for our problem. We need to trust Him for just one.

Chapter 3

MEDITATION

"May the words of my mouth and the meditations of my heart be pleasing to you, O Lord, my rock and my redeemer." (Psalm 19:14)

Recalling God's hidden word was a daily source of encouragement to me in the hospital. Memorized scriptures from even my childhood brought peace. However, there were some moments during my recovery that required a conscious effort of *meditating* on faith-filled scriptures.

I first learned about the value of scripture meditation from my husband. Early in our marriage, we often heard the societal buzzword of transcendental meditation. We served in youth ministry in Colorado Springs, Colorado, a city where gurus of this form of meditation came to visit from all over the world. Their devotion to meditation was exemplary, but their practice included mantras of false gods and demons at their core. Unfortunately, transcendental meditation captured the world's attention at that time and still is prevalent today. However, *scripture* meditation is a life-changing practice that transcends what the world offers, enriches the spirit, and it defeats the enemy's strategies. Meditation made all the difference in Tom's life.

During our first several years of marriage, Tom often felt defeated and suffered from depression. Sometimes when I entered a room where he was sitting, I could sense the heaviness associated with depression, and I prayed about it continually. Tom loved the Lord and faithfully served Him but struggled in this one area of his life. One day he discovered the book by Dr. Tim LaHaye, *How to Win Over Depression,*[1] and everything changed.

Tom took the Personality Test mentioned in the book and received a response from Dr. LaHaye. He discovered that he was 80% melancholy, like many good Italians, which explained the tendency for depression and the emotional roller coaster he often experienced. Dr. LaHaye's letter challenged Tom with some practices he could incorporate to overcome his personality negatives and triumph in the many positives. One such method was that of scripture meditation. This one tool allowed him to conquer negative thoughts and self-pity, and his life changed dramatically. To this day, Tom is free from depression because scripture meditation is part of his daily life. During this challenging time in my life, I, too, needed to put into practice this powerful tool in a more significant way.

Several weeks before I became sick, I participated in online training for mentoring new missionaries. All ten sessions helped prepare me as a mentor, but one particular session held a key that carried me through the many tough days ahead. Our instructor conveyed a method of scripture meditation by Dr. Mark Batterson, lead pastor of National Community Church in Washington, DC., that spoke to my heart and blessed me on many levels. It is the practice of taking one scripture verse and unpacking it word by word, praying about its meaning, and applying it to our lives.

Pastor Batterson explains meditation in his book *Primal. A Quest for the Lost Soul of Christianity*: "We are what we read. But let me take it one step further. Reading without meditating is like eating without digesting. If you want to absorb the nutrients, you can't just read it; you've got to chew on it. Meditation is the way we metabolize Scripture. That's how it gets into our soul."[2]

He shared this example of scripture meditation on Facebook: "BE. Be STILL. Be still and KNOW. Be still and know that I AM GOD.' I share a simple BIBLE STUDY TECHNIQUE that helps me not just read through but PRAY THROUGH Scripture."[3] How do I just *be?* Lord, reveal to me how to be. What does it mean to be *still?* In this fast-paced world, please show me how to be still. And on it goes.

During the early days in the hospital, the Lord brought this form of meditation to my mind. I concentrated on the exercise for hours at a time, recalling the dozens of verses I committed to memory with my mother's encouragement when I was young. I will never exhaust the possibilities and exploration that this excellent meditation tool delivers, and I agree with the psalmist, "God's works are so great, worth a lifetime of study—endless enjoyment!" (Psalm 112:2, MSG)

The Psalms most aptly portray the ups and downs of David and the other writers in their walk with God. Highlighted in many of them is the need for meditation on God's Word, with Psalm 119 alone mentioning it eight times. David had a handle on meditation, and his Psalms throughout encourage us to practice it.

"Oh, the joys of those who do not follow the advice of the wicked, or stand around with sinners, or join in with mockers. But they delight in the law of the Lord, meditating on it day and night. They are like trees planted along the riverbank, bearing fruit each season. Their leaves never wither, and they prosper in all they do."(Psalm 1:1-3) If we want to find victory in the trials we face, prosper, and be successful, let our counsel come from Him, His Word. Meditate on it. Get it deep within our hearts so that when we need helpful advice, we can reach down into our roots saturated with His Word, and bring forth His counsel for our lives. Often other believers come along to encourage, inspire, and give confirmation of His counsel, quoting scriptures that reinforce what He is speaking to us.

On one particularly challenging day after the removal of the ventilator, Tom texted a scripture verse to encourage me, and I felt stirred to meditate on it. Abraham, one of the Old Testament heroes mentioned in Hebrews 11, was a man who trusted God. He wasn't included in this chapter because he was wealthy and influential or because of his engaging personality. Abraham's faith had nothing to do with himself, but it was all about God, the one he trusted. Without any children of his own, Abraham was told by God that he would be the father of nations. In his own thinking, this was impossible, yet he believed! He didn't look at his age, the age of Sarah, and the unlikelihood of offspring. Although Sarah had her moment of wavering, Abraham believed without hesitancy in the God who "...calls things that are not as though they were." (Romans 4:17, NIV)

I spent considerable time unpacking and praying through this short phrase from verse 17 that Tom sent to me. *Calls* - a deliberate, verbal action, out loud. *Things* - anything, everything, unlimited possibilities. *That are not* - have not yet existed, not yet realized, unseen. *As though they were* - already in existence, in the now, tangible.

I repeated Romans 4:17 and meditated on it again and again over the next few weeks. The moment doubt of my healing would raise its ugly head, and yes, it often did, I moved into an agreement with God, *calling those things that are not as though they were!* Still today, I say it out loud when my faith wavers. I am blessed every time I decide to live not by what I can see but by what God says is so, and He would know.

Chapter 4

BREATH FROM HEAVEN

"For the Spirit of God has made me, and the breath of the Almighty gives me life." Job 33:4

Focus

From the beginning of my hospital stay, the measure of oxygen in my blood was of prime importance. At first, it was monitored 24/7 by a finger device called an oximeter, and often blood was taken to evaluate it for even more accurate oxygen readings. When I moved from the ventilator and ICU to a regular COVID-19 recovery room, oxygen was measured periodically throughout the day and night and recorded. *The importance of this measurement did not escape my attention.*

I sensed God's presence and undergirding throughout my sickness, but I also realized that the enemy of my soul was there to hinder me. Slowly, I began to focus on the importance of this measurement and became anxious to the point where one of the nurses asked if I was worried about something or if I was uncomfortable. When she left my room, I silently prayed for the Lord to give me peace and help me change my focus.

I remember a movie from several years ago about a bride who left several grooms at the altar because she got cold feet and ran away, hence the title, *Runaway Bride*.[1] The last and final groom devised a plan through eye contact as she walked down the aisle to keep her feet from running. It was a great plan, and all was going well until a camera flashed, she lost eye contact with the groom, and yes, she headed for the hills. As with most romantic comedies, they eventually got married and lived happily ever after, but the movie provides a great example of what can happen when we get distracted and lose our focus.

The story found in Deuteronomy of the charge given by Israel's great leader Moses to possess the Promised Land has always been inspiring to me. Standing at the edge of their long-sought victory, the Israelites were instructed by Moses, "*Do not be afraid* as you go out to fight your enemies today! Do not lose heart or panic or tremble before them. For the Lord your God is going with you! He will fight for you against your enemies, and He will give you victory!" (Deuteronomy 20:3-4, emphasis added) Moses then urged his officers to release all those who were distracted by the cares of this life (verse 7). *Focus* is a powerful tool in our battle against the enemy as we follow our leader to victory, but distractions hamper both our focus and resolve. Another concern of Moses was that of *fear*. "Is anyone here afraid or worried? If you are, you may go home before you frighten anyone else." (verse 8)

The advice Moses gave that day as the Israelites sat poised for victory in the Promised Land was advice that we should take to heart when we face any battle. Whether in the area of health, relationships, finances, or *anything*, success will come when we keep our *focus* on the Lord and remember His faithfulness, trust Him, and not be afraid. I've heard it said that allowing fear in our lives is like running from something that isn't chasing us, a wasted effort to be sure. *Fear has never been, nor will it ever be, a good advisor.*

Just as the enemy brought fear to the Israelites years before at their first attempt to enter Canaan, our enemy is on the offensive to bring fear and discouragement to us. He sat ready to distract me with suppositions about my oxygen levels – why are my levels not improving, what if they don't improve, and will I ever leave the hospital? We learn in the book of Job, Chapter 1, all about the enemy's tactics. Even standing before God, he spreads his lies and accusations about us. Jesus warned His followers in John 8:44, speaking of the Devil, "He was a killer from the very start. He couldn't stand the truth because there wasn't a shred of truth in him. When the Liar speaks, he makes it up out of his lying nature and fills the world with lies." (MSG) Why would I listen to him, the one who can't tell the truth! Thankfully, the Lord's presence once again filled my hospital room, and I *realized* I was distracted. I had lost my focus, and fear was standing at the door. However, the Lord was right there to change my focus.

Our Role

Psalm 43:5 states both the question and answer to the dilemma I was facing, "Why are you down in the dumps, dear soul? Why are you crying the blues? *Fix my eyes on God*—soon I'll be praising again. He puts a smile on my face. He's my God." (MSG, emphasis added)

The psalmist in Psalm 123:1-2 also penned the solution to my problem. "I lift my eyes to you, O God, enthroned in heaven. We *keep looking to the Lord our God* for his mercy, just as servants keep their eyes on their master, as a slave girl watches her mistress for the slightest signal." (emphasis added) Servants stand ready to move, like runners at the block, anticipating the signal to run, to fetch, to do for the master. Shifting their eyes away could cause them to miss the awaited signal, the chance *to serve, or* even *receive from the master's generous hand.* It's all about focus.

Whenever I faced a difficult situation in my youth, my mom always said, "Phyllis, you can't look at circumstances. You have to keep your eyes on Jesus." And how right she was! Every time I focused on the problem, I lost sight of my Master and His hand of mercy for the solution. When we keep our eyes fixed on Him, just like the servant fixed on his master, we won't miss anything God has for us, and we won't yield to the enemy's temptations.

In Acts 7, Stephen knew where to keep his focus as the stones were flying. "But Stephen, full of the Holy Spirit, gazed steadily into heaven and saw the glory of God, and he saw Jesus standing in the place of honor at

God's right hand." (Acts 7:55) Stephen's darkest moment became a glorious light as he looked to God for help. Hebrews 12:1-2 urges us, "Let us run with endurance the race God has set before us. We do this by keeping our eyes on Jesus, the champion who initiates and perfects our faith." He's our Master who signals, initiates, and perfects our faith and the actions we take with that faith. When we focus on Him, the enemy is powerless.

Dr. Caroline Leaf has written extensively about the effects our thought life and focus have on our daily life. In *Switch On Your Brain: The Key to Peak Happiness, Thinking, and Health,* she writes, "What you are thinking every moment of every day becomes a physical reality in your brain and body, which affects your optimal mental and physical health. These thoughts collectively form your attitude, which is your state of mind, and it's your attitude and not your DNA that determines much of the quality of your life."[2] In her book, she also writes, "I want to shape my world around God's truth because I know as a scientist and a believer, paying attention to my thoughts and purposefully focusing my mind leads to great transformations."[3]

According to Dr. Leaf, our thought pattern changes the brain's function, which affects the health of our body. Our role in response to any struggle is to tenaciously focus on the Lord and His limitless power to help us in all circumstances of life. And the best news I have to offer is that we are not alone in our focus struggle—He is with us!

God's Role

In response to my hospital bed prayer, the Lord brought to my mind the chorus of an old hymn, written in 1920 by G.T. Haywood, an unusual song for someone in my circumstance. I've always considered that its message referred to salvation rather than to one of comfort. I hadn't thought of it for over 35 years, yet the words flowed with ease one morning in the early stages of my illness:

> I see a crimson stream of blood,
> It flows from Calvary,
> *Its waves which reach the throne of God,*
> *Are sweeping over me.*[4]

I envisioned Calvary's waves of cleansing and healing sweeping over me straight from *God's throne,* carrying with them the *breath* from Heaven. It seemed like each *wave from Calvary* brought oxygen to my labored breathing, and God's peace instantly enveloped me. I sang it again and again in my mind with hope and peace mounting each time. I believe Heaven's angel choir joined me in song in that room of seclusion and despair, and the atmosphere changed! Later I learned that when a dear friend and her family were praying for me during this time, her mother-in-law saw angels all around me and declared, "Don't worry, she will be ok, she has special care." And I did.

Although the oxygen measurements continued throughout the rest of my recovery in the hospital, I experienced abiding peace all through the process. Every so often, I closed my eyes and sensed the waves from His throne sweeping over me. The anxiety was gone and replaced with His peace.

Our God is supernatural in His dealings with us. Why this salvation song from so long ago? I don't know. I can think of a hundred contemporary songs about healing, peace, and hope. Yet, this old song changed my world at that moment. It was supernatural, and it was nothing any man could devise.

In the depths of our suffering, our best response is to call out to the One who can supernaturally change our *focus* or *situation.* I wanted my *circumstance* changed, I wanted healing at that moment, and I wanted to walk out of the hospital. When the supernatural is involved, anything can happen! However, for that moment, God chose to change my *focus.* Would I choose to trust my Creator? The One who knows me best, the One who knows my future? How could I not trust Him!

Focusing on oxygen measurements no longer filled my mind. I was receiving a supernatural *breath from Heaven,* and it carried me along until the oxygen measurements were sufficient to release me from the hospital. Our focus affects the path our thought-life travels.

"He's solid rock under my feet, *breathing room for my soul. . .*" (Psalm 62:2, MSG, emphasis added)

Chapter 5

SONGS IN THE NIGHT

"I lie awake thinking of you, meditating on you through the night. Because you are my helper, I sing for joy in the shadow of your wings." (Psalm 63:6-7)

Early in my hospital stay, my room had no window to the outside, and I didn't know if it was day or night. At first, this lack of awareness troubled me, but like many other questions, I had to let it go. And really, what did it matter? I was restrained and obviously not going anywhere anytime soon. However, God's presence was with me, helping pass the time with delightful solutions to my restraint, whether day or night.

As I've mentioned, recalling scriptures and meditation were invaluable to me. The supernatural blessing of remembering the old hymn, "I See A Crimson Stream of Blood," changed my focus and renewed my hope. But in addition, at times there came a spontaneous eruption of praise and worship songs that rocked my world. I couldn't sing them out loud because I didn't have the breath to do so, but they sang loud and clear in my mind. I'm confident the Lord instigated these concerts.

My heart and mind filled with a variety of old choruses and contemporary praise and worship songs, and all were a blessing that helped pass the hours. Singing about the One who knew me best, loved me most, and could hear my silent song encouraged my heart. No one could understand the position I was in more than the Psalmist David.

Something to Sing About

Many believe David wrote Psalm 63 while hiding from those involved in Absalom's rebellion seeking to kill him. Away from home, lonely and vulnerable, David could think of only one comfort, and that was his God. Now I found myself in this position, where God was the only comfort and sure solution to my illness, isolation, and fear.

Like me, David did not have an immediate answer to his dilemma, so he focused on what he *did* have. He had his *God*, "I have seen you in your sanctuary and gazed upon your power and glory." (Psalm 63:2) He had his *song*, "I will praise you as long as I live, and in your name I will lift up my hands...with singing lips my mouth will praise you." (63:4-5). And he had his *joy*, "Because you are my helper, I sing for joy in the shadow of your wings." (63:7) We may find ourselves in a situation that may not be anything to sing a joyful song about, but we have our God, and He alone is *something to sing about!*

"I lie awake thinking of you, meditating on you through the night. Because you are my helper, I sing for joy in the shadow of your wings. I cling to you; your strong right hand holds me securely." (Psalm 63:6-8) With sleep often just out of my grasp, the many hours, regardless of day or night, could have been unbearable. Counting sheep may have been helpful, but I chose to *count* on the Shepherd. "I lie awake thinking of You, meditating on You through the night," the One who has helped me in times past, the One who knows the future, the One who loves me, the One who fills me with *songs in the night*.

"I Will Wake the Dawn with My Song"

"My heart is *confident* in you, O God; no wonder I can sing your praises with all my heart! Wake up, lyre and harp! *I will wake the dawn with my song.*" (Psalm 108:1-2)

My college friend, Judy McEachran, was a special blessing during the weeks of my illness. We hadn't seen each other for decades and only recently connected through Facebook, but she was praying for me. Judy is an outstanding pianist, and she sent me a beautiful online rendition of "I See A Crimson Stream of Blood" soon after I returned home from the hospital. What a blessing! A few weeks later, during a challenging time in my recovery, she felt to send her arrangement of "I Am Thine, Oh Lord." For many days following, I would *wake the dawn* with this song of commitment to the Lord on my mind. "Draw me nearer, nearer blessed Lord...O the pure delight of a single hour that before thy throne I spend, When I kneel in prayer, and with Thee, my God, I commune as friend with friend!"[1]

I must admit I started a few days during recovery with my joy tested. Even when I could sleep, my first thoughts and feelings of the day *overwhelmed* me at times. My doctor said this was a common side effect for patients who suffered from a severe infection of the virus. Regardless, attempting to kick-start the day in this way is like biking uphill – it's hard work. David expressed the best way to start the day in Psalm 108. He woke up *confident*, not in himself, but confident in the One who *gave* him the day and exclaimed in Psalm 118:24, "This is the day the Lord has made. We will rejoice and be glad in it." This declaration is how I want to start each day.

Having nothing to do with the creation of each day, I understand it is only through God's merciful plan for my life that I have breath. If He found the day valuable enough to give it to me, through a miracle healing I must add, then, of course, I am thankful for it regardless of the hardship that may exist. David, who certainly knew his share of challenges, woke the day in Psalm 108 with *thankful singing*, "I will thank you, Lord, among all the people. I will sing your praises among the nation." (Psalm 108:3) And he woke up *praising,* "For your unfailing love is higher than the heavens. Your faithfulness reaches to the clouds. Be exalted, O God, above the highest heavens. May your glory shine over all the earth." (Psalm 108:4-5)

Whether our night is passed with restful sleep or filled with thoughts and songs about our Lord, there's just no room for gloom or doom at the start of our day. I had to turn my anxious, negative waking thoughts to the Lord, thank Him for another day to spend with Him, and praise Him for His greatness. When we start our day in this way, focused on Him, the challenges we face are placed under the Lord's watchful care. The best way to start every day!

Chapter 6

GET YOUR PRAISE ON!

"My mouth is filled with God's praise. Let everything living bless him, bless his holy name from now to eternity!" (Psalm 145:21, MSG)

We quickly learn in our walk with the Lord about the *power of praise* in our lives. Talk about a focus changer! As I explained earlier, to maintain peace in my heart in the hospital, I had to turn my focus away from monitoring and hours of isolation. Not only was this true during the long nights but also throughout the day. Thankfully, I remembered how to do just that.

A few years ago, while going through a difficult situation, I felt like I was carrying the weight of the world on my shoulders, and apparently, I looked like it. A friend of mine looked at me and said something to the effect, "Phyllis, you've got to *get your praise on.*" While the trials I faced that day were nothing to bring on a shout, I turned my focus from those challenges to the faithfulness of the Lord, and everything changed.

Consider His Greatness

"Come, let us sing to the Lord! Let us *shout joyfully* to the Rock of our salvation. Let us come to him with thanksgiving. Let us sing psalms of praise to him. For the Lord is a great God, a great King above all gods." (Psalm 95:1-3, emphasis added) When we think about God's greatness, there's so much praise to give Him that sometimes we want to get *rowdy* with it, *joyfully shouting* because of our salvation, because He alone changed everything for us. If we genuinely *consider* this fact, it's hard to contain or hold our joy, so why do we often do just that – *contain* our joy? Maybe we're not taking the time to *consider* His greatness. Yet, I knew that's what I needed to do to keep peace in my heart during my many days of illness. I didn't have the strength to shout with exuberance, but I shouted in my heart for all of heaven to hear.

I started to thank Him for my salvation and His goodness to me. I praised Him for who He was, *a great God, a great King above all kings* with the resources of the universe at His disposal. After all, "He holds in his hands the depths of the earth and the mightiest mountains. The sea belongs to him, for he made it. His hands formed the dry land, too." (Psalm 95:4-5) Whenever I praised Him, my circumstances had not changed, but the *weight* of them lifted, and I felt 50 pounds lighter, something, of course, I always like to feel.

Occasionally during these times of praise, my heart became quiet. I found no words to say and could only pause in His Holy presence as peace and rest flooded my being that nothing else, no substitute, could ever bring. "Come, let us *worship and bow down*. Let us kneel before the Lord our maker, for he is our God. We are the people he watches over, the *flock under his care*." (Psalm 95:6-7, emphasis added) Tucked there under the folds of my Shepherd's garment and humbled by the knowledge that He was taking care of all my concerns, I remembered that, "The Lord is my Shepherd; I shall not want..." (Psalm 23:1, KJV) Tears streamed down my face often as I worshiped the greatness of my God, and peace always followed.

A Sacrifice of Praise

Just like I experienced in my hospital bed, I've had a few days in my life when everything appeared to be in turmoil, and all I could see was the negative side of life. In situations like this, it's challenging to find a reason to praise, but this is when we are encouraged to offer a *sacrifice* of praise. We can offer praise because of everything Jesus has done for us. In Hebrews 13:15, we are urged, "Let us offer through Jesus a continual sacrifice of praise to God..." We place our negatives at the foot of the cross and praise Him regardless of how we feel, a sacrifice of praise.

David's life is a valuable source of inspiration to turn to when facing difficulties. Although he frequently expresses his trouble and discouragement in the Psalms, he most often manages to end his laments with praise. In Psalm 103, David gives many reasons to praise the Lord,

"O my soul, bless God. From head to toe, I'll bless his holy name! O my soul, bless God, don't forget a single blessing! He *forgives* your sins—every one. He *heals* your diseases—every one. He *redeems* you from hell—saves your life! He *crowns* you with love and mercy—a paradise crown. He *wraps* you in goodness—beauty eternal. He *renews* your youth—*you're always young* in his presence." (Psalm 103:3-5, MSG, emphasis added) And the Psalm goes on to exalt the goodness of God. To always be young in His presence is reason enough for me to *get my praise on!*

Regardless of what we are walking through, there is always something good that can stir us to praise the Lord. We just need to shift our focus from our problems to our God. In the event we need a reminder, David thoughtfully supplied us in Psalm 145:8-20 with a long list of suggestions that encourage us to praise:

- "The Lord is merciful and compassionate,
- Slow to get angry
- And filled with unfailing love.
- The Lord is good to everyone.
- He showers compassion on all his creation.
- All of your works will thank you, Lord,
- And your faithful followers will praise you.
- They will speak of the glory of your kingdom;
- They will give examples of your power.
- They will tell about your mighty deeds
- And about the majesty and glory of your reign.
- For your kingdom is an everlasting kingdom.
- You rule throughout all generations.
- The Lord always keeps his promises;

- He is gracious in all he does.
- The Lord helps the fallen
- And lifts those bent beneath their loads.
- The eyes of all look to you in hope;
- You give them their food as they need it.
- When you open your hand, you satisfy the hunger and thirst of every living thing.
- The Lord is righteous in everything he does;
- He is filled with kindness.
- The Lord is close to all who call on him, yes, to all who call on him in truth.
- He grants the desires of those who fear him;
- Hears their cries for help and rescues them.
- The Lord protects all those who love him, but he destroys the wicked."

David's list will keep us busy praising! A special blessing comes when we *meditate* on these tremendous attributes of the Lord and personalize them. He *always keeps His promises to me*. He *heard my cry and rescued me* when I was at death's door.

The last verse of the last Psalm in the Book of Psalms declares, "Let every living, breathing creature praise God! Hallelujah!" (Psalm 150:6, MSG) And with what little breath I had, I knew I had to praise Him *through* the challenges I faced in the hospital. I had to *get my praise on!*

Chapter 7

FAITH WINS!

"Now faith is being sure of what we hope for and certain of what we do not see." (Hebrews 11:1)

While God developed my faith in the hospital through scripture, meditation, and praise, He was filling Tom and those who were praying for me with faith to believe for my complete healing.

"Good Report from the doctor at 16:00 today, 3-25-20. The ventilator is giving plenty of oxygen. I'm very encouraged. Also, hydroxychloroquine is working as well. Thank you for your continued prayer for Phyllis. FAITH WINS, ALWAYS IN THE PAST, ALWAYS IN THE FUTURE AND ALWAYS NOW!"

This post from Tom on Facebook began a campaign to believe for my healing, to believe for anything! Those following him on Facebook copied "Faith Wins" and passed it along on their own Facebook pages. Within a few minutes, the phrase traveled around the world via Tom's 5000 friends and friends of friends.

As I travel and speak in churches, I'm often approached, even as I enter the front door, by a joyful, "You're here! We've prayed for you! Praise the Lord." I repeatedly hear from believers how God's touch on my life has increased their faith to believe for the impossible. It was this faith that carried Tom along when the doctor reports were discouraging during the early days of my hospitalization. He clung just as I did to the scripture verse he shared with me early on, Romans 4:17, "The God who gives life to the dead and *calls things that are not as though they were.*" (NIV, emphasis added)

FAITH WINS, ALWAYS IN THE PAST, ALWAYS IN THE FUTURE AND ALWAYS NOW!"

Giants in the Land

Tom's post from March 26 - "Phyllis update 3-26-20: The 3 pm report today is good. The doctor said that her inflammation is down, and her kidney function is good. He said that she would be on the ventilator a few more days but progress today is good.

"That is encouraging to me. Others have had kidney complications so what a blessing it is that her kidneys are functioning well. So could I say again that *even if the report was bad,* FAITH WINS!

"And I love to say Romans 8:11. It says, 'And if the Spirit of him who raised Jesus from the dead is living in you,' and I like to stop and say, AND HE DOES, 'he who raised Christ from the dead will also give life to your mortal bodies because of his Spirit who lives in you.' (NIV) THANK YOU FOR BELIEVING AND PRAYING!"

I love Tom's heart. "Even if the report was bad, faith wins!" Although Tom was hoping to hear that the doctor had removed the ventilator, he focused on the positive—my kidneys were functioning well. He ignored the *giant* in the room—remaining on the ventilator for a few more days—and focused on the positive report.

"We entered the land you sent us to explore, and it is indeed a bountiful country—a land flowing with milk and honey. Here is the kind of fruit it produces. *But* the people living there are powerful, and their towns are large and fortified. We even saw giants there, the descendants of Anak!…We can't go up there against them! They are stronger than we are!' So they spread this bad report about the land among the Israelites." (Number 13:27-32, emphasis added) The children of Israel stood at the threshold of occupying their promised land, yet allowed the little word *but* to keep them from it.

It's not easy to look past the giants looming in our lives. I remember when my granddaughter, Giana, learned the word *humongous* while watching Sesame Street and used it with great excitement whenever she saw something she considered really large. I can't help but think of her when I read this story of the twelve spies. The spies returned to the Israelite camp with a *humongous* cluster of grapes so large that *two* men had to carry it, but, unfortunately, all they remembered were the *humongous* giants in the land.

Listed in Numbers 13 are the names of all twelve men who spied out the land, but of those names, we only remember *two* of them. The others are all very forgettable. When positioned to step into God's destiny for us, we can easily lose sight of it if we focus on the humongous obstacles in front of us instead of His promises. Those grapes were huge and represented God's promise of a land flowing with milk and honey, rich and abundant.

Joshua and Caleb were impressed by the grapes, not by the giants. "They said to all the people of Israel, 'The land we traveled through and explored is a wonderful land! And if the Lord is pleased with us, he will bring us safely into that land and give it to us. It is a rich land flowing with milk and honey. Do not rebel against the Lord, and don't be afraid of the people of the land. They are only helpless prey to us! They have no protection, but the Lord is with us! Don't be afraid of them!'" (Numbers 14:7-9). Just like Joshua and Caleb, Tom focused on the promises from God on my behalf and not on the giant.

When we are on the edge of something wonderful that God has planned for us, we want the faith of Joshua and Caleb and not the doubt of the fearful spies. God will never promise something impossible to attain because all things are possible with Him. Of all the Israelites standing in the camp on that day, only Joshua and Caleb entered the Promised Land to receive God's *humongous* blessing.

I don't want to miss all that God has for me because of obstacles that I perceive to be bigger than they are. I want to be like Joshua and Caleb, who, through eyes of faith, saw the huge blessing God had waiting for them. Faith wins!

Amazing Faith

"Doctor's update 3 pm, 3-27-20: Doctor said the Phyllis' blood inflammation continues to go down. The hydroxychloroquine treatment has gone well. The only issue is that she is experiencing *anxiety* from the medicine they are using for the ventilator. Pray with me Romans 8:15. All in all, a good report! I am encouraged! FAITH WINS!!"

Romans 8:15 states, "For you did not receive a spirit that makes you a slave again to fear, but you received the Spirit of sonship. And by him we cry, *'Abba,* Father.'" (NIV) As God's children, we have no excuse to entertain fear, regardless of the reports. *Anxiety* was a toxic word to Tom with the ability to cause fear because of his cousin's experience mentioned in Chapter 1. Still, he refused to accept the agenda that word carried. Instead, he remembered whose son he was and wisely chose to *trust*.

"Trust in the Lord with all your heart; do not depend on your own understanding. Seek His will in all you do, and He will show you which path to take. Don't be impressed with your own wisdom." (Proverbs 3:5-7) We may say that we have *faith*, but it's the act of *trust* that applies the action to our faith. Faith without trust is like knowledge without wisdom—great to possess but not as useful as it could be. When I depend on my own understanding, there's really only one person to trust in, and that's me—not very wise when the wisdom of heaven is mine for the asking.

One of the best illustrations in the New Testament of action demonstrating faith is the story found in Luke 7 of the Roman officer whose valued servant was ill. He had heard about the authority over sickness that a Jewish man named Jesus possessed, and military people understand authority. "Lord, don't trouble yourself by coming to my home, for I am not worthy of such an honor. I am not even worthy to come and meet you. *Just say the word* from where you are, and my servant will be healed…When Jesus heard this, *He was amazed*. Turning to the crowd that was following Him, He said, 'I tell you, I haven't seen faith like this in all Israel.'" (Luke 7:6-9, emphasis added) *Amazing Jesus!* Well, it's true—He certainly is amazing. But I mean amazing in a sense to amaze Jesus. Every time I read this story, I question, *Has my faith ever amazed Jesus?*

"Just say the word from where you are, and my servant will be healed. I know this because I am under the authority of my superior officers, and I have authority over my soldiers, I only need to say 'Go,' and they go or 'Come,' and they come." (Luke 7:7-8) From the accounts he had heard, the officer understood the authority that Jesus possessed over sickness and death, and he believed it! Then, he demonstrated his trust in Jesus with his actions. Having read all the miracles of Jesus throughout the Gospels, do I have the faith of the Roman officer?

I wonder if the thing that thrilled Jesus the most was that the man understood that healing from Him did not require a special potion, a particular location, or standing on his left foot and counting to 100. "Just say the word," was all it took. Just say the word. Trust.

In Luke 7 and 8, we learn that Jesus ministered to the undesirables of His day when He responded to a gentile officer, forgave an immoral woman, delivered a demoniac, and healed an unclean woman. Apparently, His miracles did not fall under the scrutiny of racial or moral profiling—everyone and everything are under His authority!

We have heard of His miraculous works, but do we *amaze* Him with our faith and trust that He will heal our bodies, set people free, and provide the jobs, food, and shelter that we need. The method Jesus uses to respond to our requests is in His hands, but the miracle often begins when our faith, demonstrated by our actions, catches His attention. Oh, how I want to amaze Him!

I believe Tom's faith was put to the test during my illness. He chose to demonstrate his faith with continual words and actions of affirmation regardless of setbacks and doctor reports—Faith Wins! Perhaps Tom's faith amazed the Lord.

Tenacious Faith

"ANOTHER GOOD REPORT TODAY 3-28-20: The doctor said that Phyllis is stable and that there does not seem to be any anxiety today. What great news! Her breathing is relaxed and getting stronger. I don't know when they can take her off the ventilator, but she is trying to breathe on her own. That is good. This is the last day of the hydroxychloroquine/azithromycin treatment, and she has progressed every day on that treatment.

"Thank you for praying. It is making a big difference. I wish I could say more, but that is today's report...Let's keep Believing!! FAITH ALWAYS WINS, HEBREWS 11:1! TOM"

"Now faith is being sure of what we hope for and certain of what we do not see." (Hebrews 11:1, NIV) Being *certain* of something gives us the tenacity to move forward with confidence. Tom exhibited this confidence to me every day during my illness in the hospital and my recovery at home. I know God used him to bring encouragement to me when I lacked confidence on my own. He was certain of my healing and never gave up. He was persistent!

Do or die, now or never, win or lose, all or nothing! This is the language and motivation of those who plan to succeed, who put their heads down and charge. We all know individuals who live at this level of determination. *Persistence* is the quality of continuing despite challenges or difficulties, and *determination* is a commitment to a goal or intention. Both of these are characteristics of people who know how to get the job done. Some people are born with this drive, while others develop it out of great need. The latter was Tom's incentive, and, more than likely, it was the driving force for the desperate woman found in Mark 5. With an attitude of all or nothing, something happened for her.

"A woman in the crowd had suffered for twelve years with constant bleeding. She had suffered a great deal from many doctors, and over the years she had spent everything she had to pay them, but she had gotten no better. In fact, she had gotten worse. She had heard about

Jesus, so she came up behind him through the crowd and touched his robe. For she thought to herself, 'If I can just touch his robe, I will be healed.' Immediately the bleeding stopped, and she could feel in her body that she had been healed of her terrible condition." (Mark 5:25-29) Do or die!

This dear woman had gone through the proper channels to get well, but they had failed her. Now it was time to put her head down and charge, and charge she did, right through the crowd surrounding her target and right through the many obstacles she faced: *She was a woman.* Approaching a religious teacher was not acceptable in her day. *She was unclean.* Her bleeding issue labeled her impure in the eyes of others. *She was sick.* Weak and sickly from her disease made her approach to Him a significant challenge. *Movement through the crowd was difficult.* Everyone wanted to get close to this great Teacher.

In the early days of the virus, I lacked the strength and drive that this woman seemed to possess. Thankfully, Tom carried it for me, as expressed in his post, "Let's keep Believing!! FAITH ALWAYS WINS." The woman's determination, as well as Tom's, cause me to question: Are we as resolute to see our needs met by the Lord as this tenacious woman was? Do or die? All or nothing? Fight every demon in hell to win? Or do we allow what people think or our place in society to stop us? Do we push past the people who say there is no answer? Do we push through the pain of our situation to touch Jesus the Healer, the Shepherd, the Provider?

I've always been encouraged by the permission granted in Hebrews 4:16, "So let us come boldly to the throne of our gracious God. There we will receive his mercy, and we will find grace to help us when we need it most." In other words, don't stay back in the crowd and wonder if it would be acceptable, don't be hindered by the press of the crowd or the challenge of our need. When we boldly go to the throne of our gracious God, we, too, will see our needs met.

"Daughter, your faith has made you well. Go in peace. Your suffering is over." (Mark 5:34) When Jesus asked who had touched Him, it wasn't to chastise but to tell her that it wasn't His garment that made her well. Many had touched Him that day. No, it was her *faith* in His healing virtue that got His attention. Persistent determination brought her faith to the attention of the Healer.

I hear over and over from many individuals how Tom's Facebook posts of faith and determination encouraged them not only for my healing but also for the challenges they were facing with health, family, and a myriad of issues. For Tom, *faith wins* is not just something to say to encourage others. It's a determination from deep within his spirit.

Faith conquers the *giants* we face, carries the potential of *amazing* Jesus, drives our determination to touch Him, and without it, it's impossible to please the Lord. Tom's commitment to speaking faith was contagious, and God used it to build mine when it wavered.

Fixed to the Rock—faith always wins!

Tom texted the following lyrics to me just before my connection to the ventilator, but the nurse had already taken my phone, and I didn't see it. Unable to even hold a phone the first couple of days after the ventilator, I missed his message until much later. The last thing on his heart before all the uncertainties of my medically induced coma was this song. He texted:

> "My hope is built on nothing less
> Than Jesus' blood and righteousness;
> I dare not trust the sweetest frame,
> But wholly lean on Jesus' name.
>
> Refrain:
> On Christ, the solid Rock, I stand;
> All other ground is sinking sand,
> All other ground is sinking sand.
>
> When darkness veils His lovely face,
> I rest on His unchanging grace;
> In every high and stormy gale,
> My anchor holds within the veil."[1]

This familiar hymn of assurance, "The Solid Rock," came to his mind. The Lord was Tom's sure anchor during this *stormy gale*. While the doctors were competent and knowledgeable, he dared not trust only in *the sweetest frame*, the best medical framework available, but instead secured his anchor to where he placed his faith. And to keep that anchor firmly in place, Tom called on believers everywhere, through Facebook, messaging, and phone, to pray for us.

Later, during one of the most challenging moments in my recovery at home, I discovered his text message. It was like a shot of adrenaline, and with such a random discovery, I was certain that I was on solid ground and also that our friends were still praying. I know that God led me to find it. *Our hope is built on nothing less* than the indestructible Solid Rock, the Lord Jesus! Jesus said if we build our lives on Him and His guidance, we are smart: "You are like a smart carpenter who built his house on solid rock. Rain poured down, the river flooded, a tornado hit—but nothing moved that house. It was fixed to the rock." (Matthew 7:24-25, MSG)

With the many complications from the virus I experienced during my recovery, it would have been easy to lean on the internet for information. However, through the years, I've learned that this information is not always *solid* and can produce fear rather than hope in some cases. Like a *smart carpenter*, I kept my foundation, faith, and hope on the Lord and His guidance. I was encouraged, with my faith intact. Yes, *fixed to the Rock – faith always wins!*

Chapter 8

GRATEFUL

When my attitude is one of gratitude, I can make it through anything.

Through the many circumstances I faced as a child, my mom often reminded me of God's promise found in Hebrews 13:5, "I will never leave thee, nor forsake thee." (KJV) Committed to memory, I carried this promise with me through life and shared it frequently with others. Yes, life has brought me several disappointments, but in those moments, has God ever abandoned me? Did He not walk with me, bring encouragement and guidance on every occasion?

Remembering God's faithfulness in the past brings comfort in today's struggle. He never promised a pain-free life, but He did promise to stay with us through it. Isaiah 43 comes to mind, "Fear not. . . When you pass through the waters, I will be with you; and when you pass through the rivers, they will not sweep over you. . . For I am the Lord, your God . . . your Savior; . . . you are precious and honored in my sight, and . . . I love you." (Isaiah 43:1-4, NIV)

Remembering His Faithfulness with Gratitude

To help pass the time in isolation and recovery, the Lord reminded me of His faithful care throughout my life, starting when I was just a young child. I reflected on His faithfulness for hours on end.

As a young wife and mother, my mom was very devout in her faith, attending mass every week and faithfully reciting the prayers of the rosary. However, a couple of years before I was born, she discovered a new faith in God and became a born-again believer. My dad did not share this new-found belief at the time, and when I was born, our home life was troubled.

As early as three years old, I remember watching my mom respond to my dad's anger with supernatural grace, not cowering in defeat but standing firm with the Holy Spirit's guidance. Occasionally, dad did not want us to go to church. When this happened, mom went to her prayer closet, often with my sister and me in tow, and we prayed that God would change his heart. And God *always* did. Remembering moments like this, I became enormously grateful for the example set by my mom and thankful for God's faithful response to her call for help.

Remembering His Healing Touch with Gratitude

One of my favorite accounts in the Bible that reveals a grateful heart is found in Luke 17. "As Jesus continued on toward Jerusalem, He reached the border between Galilee and Samaria. As He entered a village there, ten lepers stood at a distance, crying out, 'Jesus, Master, have mercy on us!'" (Luke 17:11-13) I must admit I would be tempted to avoid groups of *lepers* calling out to me, but not Jesus. Jesus made one request of them, "He looked at them and said, 'Go show yourselves to the priests.' And *as they went,* they were cleansed of their leprosy." (verse 14, emphasis added) Even before they saw the evidence of healing, they responded in obedience, did what He said, and because of it, they received healing.

"One of them, when he saw that he was healed, came back to Jesus, shouting, 'Praise God!' He fell to the ground at Jesus' feet, thanking Him for what He had done. This man was a Samaritan. Jesus asked, 'Didn't I heal ten men? Where are the other nine?'...And Jesus said to the man, 'Stand up and go. *Your faith has healed you.*'" (15-19, emphasis added) The nine lepers were so focused on their healing that they forgot about the Healer, but the Samaritan man who had every reason to avoid Jesus returned to give thanks.

By returning to the Healer, the man not only was healed of leprosy like the others, but he found out *why.* His grateful heart offered a face to face dialogue with Jesus, who gave him one of the keys to any future healing, *"Your faith has healed you."* However, in the original language, this word *healed* has a deeper meaning and is often translated *made whole,* speaking not only of physical healing but of spiritual healing as well. The man's belief in the Lord and His wholehearted act of giving glory to the Lord made him the victor that day.

Remembering God's healing touch with a heart of gratitude makes us victors too!

I reflected on the many occasions God healed me from stomach problems, injuries, and other ailments over the years. One such time stands out in my mind today. When I was seven, a dozen or so warts developed on my left hand, and I was embarrassed by their appearance. After several months, I went to my mom, sobbing in despair, and shared with her my feelings. She prayed for me on the spot, rebuking every one of them. The next morning, I woke up to find every wart was gone! I was stunned! Once again, God proved Himself to be the God of miracles. *Talk about grateful!* We danced and laughed with joy over God's goodness and healing power.

What gave us the faith to believe for this miracle? Perhaps it was the healing my mom received when I was baby, a miracle for sure, that she later shared with me. While raising five active children under the age of 14 plus a new baby, mom experienced persistent tonsillitis that caused pain, difficulty swallowing, fatigue, and fever. One morning, my dad looked at her throat and saw her tonsils so swollen that they were almost touching each other. Even though money was scarce, he instructed her to go to the doctor that day, and then he went to work.

Although a new believer, mom knew from reading the Bible that God could heal her body. When she found a quiet moment, she touched her throat and simply asked the Lord to heal her just as she had read in the Bible. She went about her day as best as possible and soon realized she could swallow and had more energy. By the time my dad returned home, she was completely healed. Dad looked at her throat, and with amazement, declared that her tonsils were gone, not normal in size, but gone! It seems that this bonified miracle would have brought him to repentance at that moment, but it took a few more years. Mom died at the age of 92, never experiencing those throat infections again, with two empty spaces in her throat where her tonsils had been. I looked and saw it for myself! Hearing of this miracle as a child, surely I could believe Him concerning a few warts.

Years later, when I was a young mother-to-be in the seventh month of my first pregnancy, the doctor discovered that a hormone from my baby was not showing up adequately in my bloodwork. He informed me I would be monitored closely with frequent visits to his office, and I would need to remain on bed rest until the baby was born. As a busy youth pastor's wife during the holiday season, these orders seemed impossible. We called our parents and congregation to pray about this situation and the health of our baby.

One morning as I called out in prayer to God, He directed me to Jeremiah 29:11-13. This well-known scripture has brought comfort to countless individuals, just as it did for me that day. "For I know the thoughts that I think toward you, saith the LORD, thoughts of peace, and not of evil, to give you an *expected end*. Then shall ye call upon me, and ye shall go and pray unto me, and I will hearken unto you. And ye shall seek me, and find *me*, when ye shall search for me with all your heart." (KJV, emphasis added) This *expectant* mother, seeking Him with all her heart, was healed that day and received her *expected end*. Our beautiful baby daughter, Mandy, was born three weeks early, at seven pounds, and healthy in every way. She has been a continual joy in my life from day one. I remember this moment with endless gratitude and praise God for the healing touch He brought that day.

During my weeks in the hospital, I rejoiced over dozens of occasions when God kept me from harm, guided my life, and performed miracles in our ministry, praising Him for each one. It kept me busy for long periods. *I was extremely grateful for what God had done in my past!* Little did I know as I reminisced that God was delivering me from the most significant, most destructive illness of my life to date.

Grateful in Every Situation

I chose to be grateful for my present, as well. Early in my recovery, I couldn't move and was too weak to lift even an arm. Tubes and medical equipment fed me, took care of bodily functions, and monitored me. Nurses visited regularly to remove the used items and connect the new food, medicine, etc. Once each day, they bathed me, changed my bedding all while I remained in bed, not an easy task, to be sure. It's difficult to express how humbling it was for me.

These angels of mercy never complained, but instead smiled and encouraged me through it all. They listened carefully to my questions and concerns. With Dutch as their mother tongue, they did their best to speak English. Living in a foreign country, knowing little of the language, yet cared for in this way, touched my heart and filled me with gratitude.

Because of this, I thanked the nurses and doctors for every visit and for the help they provided. Often, they responded that they were happy to do it, and sometimes it was simply *you're welcome*. They were so busy that I felt it was possibly a nuisance for them to feel the need to respond to me, but I didn't care. I was just so grateful.

When I was released from the hospital and returned home to continue healing, Tom, shared with me that our daughter and son, Mandy and Brady, and their families relentlessly prayed for my healing. They never wavered in their faith and believed for a complete recovery. I learned about the hundreds of people praying for me and the support and encouragement they gave Tom through the many days when he was alone. Colleagues from our seminary, CTS, Johanna, Dana, and Jan, brought meals to him regularly during my hospital stay and continued bringing meals for both of us when I returned home. Our dear friend, Lorna, from CTS, laundered our clothes for weeks and delivered many meals as well. Our kind downstairs neighbors brought a meal to Tom almost immediately after I was hospitalized. We will never forget the kindness of our friends during this most difficult time. I've prayed countless times for God's most abundant blessings on their lives.

To this day, I cry when I think of this army of believers praying that God would spare my life and comfort my husband. I wonder if we really understand the impact our prayers have on the heart of God, and how "The earnest prayer of a righteous person has great power and produces *wonderful results*." (James 5:16, emphasis added) Whether for physical or spiritual healing, our prayers get God's attention!

To say *I'm grateful* for these many prayers bombarding Heaven for me is inadequate because words just cannot convey my heart on the matter. I believe that Heaven recorded every prayer. So, my prayer is that God will outdo Himself blessing everyone who prayed and brought these *wonderful results.*

God Has Already Been There

I'm grateful for my future, whatever it is, and however God will use me. After a month at home recuperating, I visited my General Practitioner for the first time. Because he received a daily record of my hospital stay, he shared some sobering information with me. He said that for every week spent in the hospital, it takes one month to recover, and it was even longer for ventilator patients. During the first few months at home, I suffered from several complications, which also were a setback. I wanted to be well. I wanted to feel *normal* and do all the things I was used to doing, but I could not.

I returned home from this visit challenged by the information. The following Sunday, I listened to the online morning service from my church, Brussels Christian Center. Pastor Daniel Costanza shared a Mother's Day message about the mother of Moses, Jochebed. It was a wonderful message that touched my heart. One statement he made stood out to me, and it was a great reminder. He said Jochebed, led by God, didn't have to worry if Moses would be safe as she placed him in the reeds along the Nile's bank because God had already been there. *God had already been there!*

David grasped this marvel when he wrote in Psalm 139:1-7, "O Lord, you have examined my heart and know everything about me. You know when I sit down or stand up. You know my thoughts even when I'm far away. You see me when I travel and when I rest at home. You know everything I do. You know what I am going to say even before I say it, Lord. You go before me and follow me. You place your hand of blessing on my head. Such knowledge is too wonderful for me, too great for me to understand!"

This mystery reminds me somewhat of the Global Positioning System (GPS) that many of us use daily in our cars to guide us. I don't understand how it works, something about a satellite up in the sky? How that little box can pinpoint my location and direct me to my next destination is a mystery to me, too complicated for me to understand. Even more so and more importantly, I don't understand the omnipresence and omniscience of God, how He goes before me yet follows me, and I don't understand His desire to do so. It humbles me.

"You made all the delicate, inner parts of my body and knit me together in my mother's womb. Thank you for making me so wonderfully complex! Your workmanship is marvelous — how well I know it. You watched me as I was being formed in utter seclusion, as I was woven together in the dark of the womb. *You saw me before I was born. Every day of my life was recorded in your book. Every moment was laid out before a single day had passed."* (Psalm 139:13-16, emphasis added) How could we not trust our Creator who has been with us from our very beginning, the One who planned our course and direction and is ahead of us every step of the way?

When we're going through a difficult time, we often wonder where God is. Has He abandoned us? Sometimes our GPS is silent when we need it most because of a tunnel or obstruction. Unlike our GPS, God is infallible, but sometimes He is silent, and we question His whereabouts. David understood this questioning when he wrote, "The Lord will work out his plans for my life—for your faithful love, O Lord, endures forever. Don't abandon me, for you made me." (Psalm138:8) We can trust that God will come through for us, "I praise your name for your unfailing love and faithfulness; for your promises are backed by all the honor of your name." (Psalm 138:2) Now, that's quite a backing! GPS units like Garmin, Magellan, and TomTom may be helpful, but they don't hold a candle to the *Name of the Lord!*

From His Word, we realize that God is never surprised by our life events. He had already been in my hospital room, my recovery, and is already in my tomorrow. With all the uncertainties of the current pandemic, God has already been here. And if we know anything about our merciful God at all, we know He will guide us through it and every similar situation. He will give us the grace and wisdom to move forward into the future without fear and trepidation because *He has already been there, and His promises are backed by the honor of His Name!*

The outcome ultimately depends on us. Will we trust the One who knows our future and follow His divine guidance? We can be sure this guidance will include proclaiming truth and sharing the message of hope for the world – His Son, Jesus. As the world deals with the loss of loved ones, employment, and finances, there is a life beyond, an eternal life that promises a loss of nothing. As believers, *this message*, pandemic or not, is our mission.

Sometimes we take God's abundant blessings and guidance throughout our lives for granted or look at the seemingly perfect lives of others in comparison. The writer of Psalm 73 experienced this as well, "No doubt about it! God is good—good to good people, good to the good-hearted. *But I nearly missed it,* missed seeing his goodness. I was looking the other way, looking up to the people at the top, envying the wicked who have it made, Who have nothing to worry about, not a care in the whole wide world." (Psalm 73:1-5, MSG, emphasis added)

What I've learned in life regarding the distraction of comparison is that looks are deceiving, and we really have no idea what path others are traveling—whether righteous or ungodly. Tomorrow is another day for all of us. "When I tried to figure it out, all I got was a splitting headache...Until I entered the sanctuary of God." (Psalm 73:16-17, MSG) In *His presence,* with our focus on Him, the things that really matter become clear. I don't want to *miss seeing his goodness* in my life for any reason.

I'm grateful for a Creator who watched over me even before birth, presides in my now, and has captured my future in His view. In the dark of isolation, the Lord continually reminded me of His faithfulness, past and present. Not only did these memories fill me with gratefulness and help to pass the time, but they also gave me faith and hope. When we call on God for help, His answer brings solutions and strategies that carry us through a lifetime of challenges. And for this, I also am grateful.

Chapter 9

EARNEST PRAYER

"The earnest prayer of a righteous person has great power and produces wonderful results." (James 5:16)

On the fifth day of my hospital stay in ICU, before the ventilator, I received the following text from Tom: "You won't believe the number of people praying for you...receive the peace of God, 'Peace I leave with you; my peace I give you. I do not give to you as the world gives. Do not let your heart be troubled and do not be afraid.'" (John 14:27, NIV) I was so sick that it was difficult to respond, but I finally managed, "The struggle to breathe is more exhausting than I can describe. A couple of times, I've been tempted just to stop. Constantly receiving bad news. May all these prayers be answered today." Tom's quick response was, "Don't quit! There are so many people praying for you."

"So Many Are Praying for You"

There's just something wonderful that happens inside of me when family and friends tell me they are praying for me—if I'm discouraged, hope builds within me; if I'm sick, faith starts to mount; and if I'm fearful, peace floods my soul. My last thoughts before ventilation carried the assurance from Tom's text message that people were praying for me. I couldn't pray for myself at this moment, but Tom had it covered by engaging everyone he knew through social media and even those he had never met.

Friends sent scriptures, songs, and words of affirmation to both of us throughout the weeks ahead. Several friends sent quotes from the book I wrote several years ago, *Intimate Moments with the Shepherd – Guidance Through the Challenges of Life.* They sent them to remind me of the faithfulness of our Shepherd. When I finally could manage the use of my phone in recovery, I tried to read all these marvelous words of encouragement from so many friends. All I could do was cry, but crying took so much of my oxygen that I had to postpone reading them for a while. I don't know if we truly understand the blessing our spirit-led expressions have on those who are ill or suffering. Every one of them meant the world to me, with more value than could be assigned, and still precious today.

Prayer for Others

In recovery, I often found myself praying for those who were praying for me as the Lord brought them to mind. My time could not have been better spent than offering these prayers on behalf of others, all part of God's help and guidance through this time of isolation, I am sure. I prayed especially for my family that God would comfort them in the process of my illness, regardless of the outcome. I prayed for divine health for my loved ones and friends who were praying for me and protection from this virus. I repeatedly asked the Lord to bless them for lifting my name in prayer to Him, and I continue to pray for them today.

Through the years, I've loved praying for the needs of others with hopeful anticipation of answered prayer and observing the way our creative God brings solutions. I've learned that promising to pray for a need can be easily sabotaged by a busy life, and often those mental notes to pray for someone cannot be found as effortlessly as they once were. Keeping a prayer journal is helpful, and simply asking God to bring to our remembrance those needs we've committed to prayer also delivers results.

A specific prayer request comes my way now and then that challenges me to find the will of God in how I really should pray for that need. I understand that God is bigger than my diligence in prayer. He remembers all the requests that I forget, and He, of course, knows how to answer every one of them. However, like most believers, I take prayer seriously because I want my prayers to be the effective prayers that James mentions in James, Chapter 5.

Paul understood the importance and impact of prayer in a believer's life and focused on it in his letters. In Colossians, he wrote to a group of believers he had never met to help and encourage them to stand against an onslaught of heresy he heard was mounting in the church. In Colossians 1:9-12, Paul shared an excellent example for us of how to pray for others, whether we *remember* the exact need or not. I don't know anyone on the planet who would not appreciate someone praying this prayer on his or her behalf. When we pray for others, ask God to help them:

1) Know His plan for their lives
2) Grow in spiritual wisdom and understanding
3) Understand how to honor and please the Lord
4) Yield good fruit
5) Grow in the knowledge of who He is
6) Have endurance and patience through His great power
7) Be filled with joy and thanksgiving

As I pray for my faithful friends, I ask for these blessings on their lives, and I am confident in God's response. When we pray to God, we pray in *Jesus' name*, and Paul gave one of the most powerful endorsements of Him found anywhere in Colossians 1:15-20. This testimonial of Jesus should establish our confidence and build our faith when we pray. "Christ is the visible image of the invisible God. He existed before anything was created and is supreme over all creation...He holds all creation together...Christ is the head...Christ is the beginning...through Him God reconciled everything to Himself."

It's almost impossible to believe, yet true – *this amazing, glorious creator of all things, the Lord Jesus, hears and answers our prayers!*

For the last 30 years or so, I've included in my devotional time a specific prayer to guarantee that God hears my prayers. I start my prayer time by asking the Lord to purify my heart. It's not so much about breaking one of the Ten Commandments, although a sin of this nature surely requires repentance. This time of repentance is more about the secret things that find their way into my everyday life, things like judging others, jealousy, pride, resentment, and unforgiveness. When left unchecked, these offenses often lead to deliberate sin. The writer of Psalm 66:17-19 declares, "For I cried out to him for help, praising him as I spoke. If I had not confessed the sin in my heart, the Lord would not have listened. But God did listen! He paid attention to my prayer." As believers living under the grace of salvation, we may forget that God loves a pure heart. When I allow the Lord to reveal to me offenses such as these, He *always* is faithful to do so, which further shows His heart on the matter. When I'm praying for someone facing a crisis, I want to be sure that my *earnest* prayer is unhindered in reaching His throne. My loved ones and friends deserve nothing less.

With the air cleared with my Father, I boldly approach His throne with this understanding, "God can do anything, you know—far more than you could ever imagine or guess or request in your wildest dreams! He does it not by pushing us around but by working within us, his Spirit deeply and gently within us." (Ephesians 3:20) This scripture verse from The Message Bible, put in modern vernacular, thrills me down to my toes. I have written it on notecards and placed them around my home, and I repeated it often while in the hospital. I claim it today for every friend going through a struggle and for myself. "God can do anything, you know—far more than you could ever imagine or guess or request in your wildest dreams!"

Chapter 10

GIANA'S SONG

"Sing him songs, belt out hymns, translate his wonders into music!" (Psalm 105:2, MSG)

My children and their families prayed for me day and night as my body battled the ravages of the virus. It's impossible to express how difficult it was for them to be an ocean away from what I was experiencing. The day I left the hospital and returned to my apartment in Brussels for extended recovery, my daughter sent this song written by my 12-year-old granddaughter, Giana. She wrote it while I was connected to the ventilator.

Giana is abundantly creative in all the arts, as well as an A student in all subjects. Her artwork has won many awards over the past several years, as has her writings. She's always working on a novella or drawing pictures with pure imagination. She turned to this creativity as she processed what her *Nonna* was going through. Out of her many prayers for me, the Lord gave her a wonderful assurance that she put to song.

Already Won

I keep fighting this Battle. It rages on. It rages on.
I keep praying for guidance
for this battle to be Won, for this battle to be Won.
Layin' in my bed, praying for answers,
For this battle to be won, for this battle to be won.
Asking Him, why would you put me through this?
And He said, My Child, I think you forgot one thing.

It's already won, already won.
The victory is mine; I have the plans.
You don't have to worry, 'cause it's already won.

I say, but how can I be sure, I still feel afraid.
And He tells me, it's ok to be afraid.
Just hold on to me through this battle,
and remember in your heart,
It's already won, it's already won.
The victory is mine; I have the plans.
Just hold on to me, and you'll be alright.
It's already won.

As I read her beautiful song of God's promise, I
cried and thanked the Lord for my precious
granddaughter and her surrender to Him. I thanked Him
for the victory He promised and claimed it as done. God
gave it not only to comfort her but to comfort me as well,
my cry for help always in His sight. I read it often down
the long road to recovery, and it encouraged my heart to
hold on to God's promise given in her song. Giana

discovered at a young age how to hear from God and express His words in a meaningful way. My heart is thrilled!

Many of the hymns and worship songs we love to sing are birthed during difficult or tragic moments in the lives of their authors. John Newton, a slave trader and rebel, wrote "Amazing Grace" in 1779 in response to God's incredible mercy in saving his life during a severe storm at sea. This beloved hymn knows no denominational boundaries and expresses for all of us the amazing grace of God in our lives to save and keep us. The blind Irish monk, Dallan Forgaill, wrote "Be Thou My Vision," expressing complete dependence on the Lord's guidance. Helen Lemmel wrote the words to "Turn Your Eyes Upon Jesus" following many heartaches. The song was inspired by a tract written by Lilias Trotter, a missionary to Algeria in the late 1800s, entitled "Focused." It's one of my favorite hymns and always reminds me of where to place my focus, "Turn your eyes upon Jesus. Look full in His wonderful face, and the things of earth will grow strangely dim in the light of His glory and grace."[1]

The story of Bart Millard, as told in the movie, *I Can Only Imagine,*[2] has touched the hearts of many. Pain, abuse, and resentment shrouded Bart's life because of the treatment he received as a child from his father. Yet, through redemption and forgiveness, Bart authored the beautiful song, *I Can Only Imagine,* a blessing to all who hear it. God still speaks to us today out of the challenges we face and calls us to *translate his wonders into music.*

It's a joy to remember all the old hymns and more contemporary songs of praise and worship, but the songs that come from a profound soul-searching encounter with God are something different yet again, whether newly-authored or not. In Psalm 96:1, the psalmist declared with emphasis, "Sing a *new* song to the Lord!" I believe this Psalm does not intend *new* to mean only a song that is different or newly written, but even more so, one that is a *fresh* and up-to-the-minute response to God's goodness and greatness in our lives.

Sometimes when He displays His power and majesty in my life, it causes me to respond with a spontaneous new song that no one has ever sung before, fresh from my heart to His. Giana's song came to her in this way. It was a new *and* fresh song, heaven-inspired, in response to her sincere prayers for me. God's gift to her ministers to me even yet today!

When a new song is vibrant in our hearts and minds, the Psalm goes on to tell us what to do with it, "*Each day proclaim* the good news that He saves. *Publish* His glorious deeds *among the nations. Tell everyone* about the amazing things He does. Great is the Lord! He is most worthy of praise!" (Psalm 96:2-3, emphasis added)

Although in the hospital I didn't have the lung capacity to sing audibly, I often carried a *fresh* song inside of me. When our song is new, fresh, and up-to-the-minute, we can't help but share the good news of God's salvation and greatness with those we meet each day. I did my best to proclaim the good news and speak of His glorious deeds to the nurses, caregivers, and doctors.

When they delivered a good report to me regarding tests and monitoring, my response frequently acknowledged God's touch on my life. This response was met mostly with silence or a shrug. However, one sweet caregiver responded, "Yes, of course, He is helping you!" That made my day! Perhaps the staff was trained to react in the way they did, but it confirmed my calling as a missionary to Belgium and Europe. I pray for them often, praying that God will lift any veil from their eyes, revealing Himself to those who do not know Him. I know He loves them dearly.

When we walk through the challenges that life throws at us, I pray that our hearts remain open to God's voice. Who knows what songs He desires to birth through us to touch our lives and the world around us. Regardless of their realized destiny, may the fresh songs from heaven fill our space with God's presence. It's *Already Won!* Thank you, Giana.

"I'm about to burst with song; I can't keep quiet about you. God, my God, I can't thank you enough." (Psalm 30:12, MSG)

Chapter 11

THE LORD, MY SHEPHERD

"Even when I walk through the darkest valley, I will not be afraid, for you are close beside me." (Psalm 23:4)

After the removal of the ventilator, I spent two or three days in an unusual room. A dim light allowed me to see why I couldn't move my limbs. My arms and legs were restrained by Velcro straps, permitting only slight movement. It was extremely uncomfortable, and I wondered about the purpose of the restraint. Occasionally, I heard sounds similar to air released from brakes and felt a slight shift in my bed. Visits from the nursing staff were infrequent, but on one occasion, I asked what was happening. The nurse explained that it was a method of continual rotation, providing a safer transition after ventilation. It was in this room when I began recalling scripture verses, and doing this was a lifesaver for me. It kept me from panicking over the sounds and restraints and helped pass the long hours of solitude.

All the many scriptures I remembered were a comfort to me, but I found great solace in one of the most beloved scripture passages of all time, Psalm 23.

"The Lord is my shepherd;
I have all that I need.
He lets me rest in green meadows;
he leads me beside peaceful streams.
He renews my strength.
He guides me along right paths,
bringing honor to his name.
Even when I walk
through the darkest valley,
I will not be afraid,
for you are close beside me.
Your rod and your staff
protect and comfort me.
You prepare a feast for me
in the presence of my enemies.
You honor me by anointing my head with oil.
My cup overflows with blessings.
Surely your goodness and unfailing love
    will pursue me all the days of my life,
and I will live in the house
    of the LORD forever."

Walking through this valley of illness, I knew I was not alone because He proved over and over again that He was with me, comforting me along the way.

Little did I know during this time that our friends were sending messages to Tom containing quotations and chapter titles from the devotional book I authored several years before, *Intimate Moments with the Shepherd—Guidance Through the Challenges of Life*. They wanted him to remind me that my Shepherd was with me in my darkest moment. The book is a collection of devotionals based on visual impressions received from the Lord during my time spent with Him each morning. The visions portray the love, care, and guidance that the Good Shepherd provides for His sheep. Through the years, countless individuals have contacted me, testifying about the comfort they received while reading the devotionals, and they comfort me, too. I understood why my friends were sharing them with us during this time.

When we follow the Shepherd, we are never truly alone. The following devotionals copied from *Intimate Moments with the Shepherd* [1] remind us of the great care our Shepherd gives to us when it is most needed.

*****

Mud in Your Eye

We never know what a day will bring to us. We can be faithfully following the Shepherd, at peace with the world, and in a split second, we can have our legs knocked out from under us and find ourselves face down in the mud. Where's the justice in that? Well, life is tough, but God is faithful.

>*Dark heavy clouds hung over the flock as the Shepherd led the sheep down a muddy slope in the pouring rain. The wool of the sheep became saturated, making it extremely difficult for them to move. This was a trying situation at best, and to make matters worse, a mudslide*

enveloped several of the sheep, carried them 20 feet down the slope, and buried them.

The Shepherd guided the larger part of the flock back to the fold and quickly returned to the mudslide. Wading through the mud, He found them, one by one, and pulled each one to solid ground. He carefully cleared the mud from their faces, and soon life began to return to their limp bodies. Then, He removed the thick mud from their limbs, enabling them to walk, and led them back to the fold.

As the returning sheep entered the fold with their Shepherd, the sheep that were already there stirred with excitement. The Shepherd had brought deliverance when things looked so bleak. No wonder they followed Him.

It can be rough in the trenches. In fact, the story goes, weary soldiers coined the phrase, "Here's mud in your eye!" as they toasted to good health and safety in the trenches of World War I. The temporary spray of blinding mud was better than the full impact of the artillery that caused the spray. But regardless of our good wishes, we learn at a relatively young age that bad things can happen to good people. A single phone call, a simple action, or a thoughtless word can send us on a downward spiral of despair no matter how closely we follow the

Shepherd. At moments like these, we seldom recall the thousands of sorrows life has been spared. It's as if mud gets in our eyes, and we temporarily lose sight of our Shepherd and His power to deliver us.

When Jesus and His disciples encountered a blind man in John 9, His disciples asked Him whose sin caused this blindness. Jesus assured them that no one's sin had caused it, but that God's power was seen through the healing of the man. Then He proceeded to put mud over the eyes of the blind man, and when the mud was washed away, the man could see! The man discovered that the Lord, who created the earth, can use any part of it to exhibit His power. Mud and the tough things that life throws our way are opportunities for God to display His greatness.

What a reassurance it is when Jesus opens our eyes, and we realize that we follow a God who is right there with us in the trenches! He is faithful to deliver us, set us back on solid ground, clear away our heartaches, and walk us back to wholeness. No one understood this better than David when he wrote: "I waited patiently for the Lord to help me, and He turned to me and heard my cry. He lifted me out of the pit of despair, out of the *mud* and *mire*. He set my feet on solid ground and steadied me as I walked along. He has given me a *new song* to sing, a hymn of praise to our God. Many will see what he has done and be astounded. They will put their trust in the Lord." (Psalm 40:1-3, emphasis added)

Our difficult experiences enable us to understand the despair that others sometimes feel and allow us to offer them the hope of deliverance. The testimony of our deliverance causes others to put their trust in God. Life is tough, but God is faithful.

So, here's mud in your eye!

*****

Unreasonable Peace

As long as we follow the Shepherd, we can be certain that His enemy is also our enemy. The fact that this is true—that we have an enemy—accomplishes one favorable result. We are careful to stay close to the Shepherd when we hear the lions roaring and the wolves howling.

> *The Shepherd and the flock were in a terrible spot! A large pack of wolves had surrounded them as they rested and grazed on the shady hillside. The sheep closed in around the Shepherd as He spoke to them, but they could not hear Him because of the deafening howls of the wolves.*
>
> *Despite this predicament, the sheep were at peace, content, and unafraid. It seemed so strange, but a closer examination of the situation brought understanding. Even though they could not hear all the comforting words of the Shepherd, the sheep had fixed their sight on His face. His calm expression and His*

> *eyes of love spoke volumes to them, and
> they were at peace.*

Unreasonable peace. Just before Jewish leaders picked up stones to kill him, Stephen, an early church leader, saw a vision of the Lord Himself. Acts 7:59-60 concludes the story, "As they stoned him, Stephen *prayed*, 'Lord Jesus, receive my spirit.' He fell to his knees, shouting, 'Lord, don't charge them with this sin!' And with that, he died." New Testament missionaries Paul and Silas were severely beaten and thrown in prison, and Acts 16:25 records, "Around midnight, Paul and Silas were praying and singing hymns to God."

These are just two examples of the *unreasonable* peace God's people—Joshua, Gideon, David, Daniel, and so many others—experienced in the midst of trouble when they fixed their eyes on the Lord. It is a peace we can have when there is no *earthly* reason to have it, a phenomenon Paul described when he wrote, "And the peace of God, which *transcends all understanding*, will guard your hearts and your minds in Christ Jesus." (Philippians 4:7, NIV)

When our enemy is *howling* at us, we, too, must fix our eyes on the Shepherd's face if we want to receive this peace. But how do we see His face? We see His eyes of love through the written Word—a *portrait* of His everlasting love for us. We see the wise, caring expression on His face when we look in the mirror—a *reflection* or record of all He has done to guide us personally. Remembering His faithfulness brings peace and contentment, and we are not afraid. When we focus intently on Him, we no longer hear the howls and roars of the enemy; in fact, we may not even be aware that they exist. Such is the nature of the Shepherd's unreasonable peace.

*****

God is in Control

Natural disasters befall rich and poor, young and old alike. These tragic events are a common denominator that causes every victim to seek after the most basic needs—water, food, shelter, and clothing. With life altered, those who survive begin heading in a new direction, grateful to be alive.

> *A curious sheep followed the Shepherd on a scouting trip. The Shepherd was perusing a dry, rugged valley that would be tomorrow's journey. At first, the sheep did not mind the challenging surroundings, enthralled by the opportunity to venture off with the Shepherd. Shortly, however, it began to focus on the difficulties of the journey and bleated and grunted its complaints.*
>
> *Suddenly the Shepherd put out His hand to silence the sheep and paused to listen to the approaching sound. In an instant, He gathered the sheep in His arms and climbed to safety just as a heaving flashflood roared past them. As*

the unusual abundance of water settled into the valley, the Shepherd comforted His startled, shaking sheep and smiled to reassure it that all was well, He was in control.

The sheep witnessed an amazing act of God that day, with the course of the flock forever altered. This flooded valley was no longer a viable path for the flock, but tomorrow their Shepherd would provide a new direction for them—He is not threatened by catastrophe.

Before the flood, the sheep seemed to be complaining about everything. The road was rough and long, dry, and barren. It did not appreciate the fact that the Shepherd was present, leading, and protecting. We tend to mimic the sheep's behavior when life gets a little rough, and often complain about all the little things that upset us. We seem to lack gratitude for all the good things we possess. However, hurricanes and floods, fires, and devastating storms become a reality check for us. It is remarkable how precious a cool, clean cup of water becomes when we have nothing. How *grateful* we are for that water, so thankful to be alive! Our Shepherd is looking out for us!

Although the flash flood altered its course, the sheep was spared from injury or death, safe in the arms of the Shepherd. Unfortunately, all are not spared from the storms that wreak havoc on the earth, and some may perish. If they are followers of God, they will find themselves in His arms, at His *eternal* destination.

When we walk with God, we are sure to view His terrifying power displayed at times. Psalm 46:1-7 dramatically portrays how our awesome God controls this vast world: "God is our refuge and strength, always ready to help in times of trouble. So we will not fear, when earthquakes come...mountains crumble...nations are in chaos...kingdoms crumble...God's voice thunders and the earth melts...Be still, and know that I am God! The Lord of Heaven's Armies is here among us." And tomorrow He will provide a new direction for us. He is not threatened by catastrophe; all is well. God is in control!

*****

The Antidote to Panic

Throat closes, pulse accelerates, stomach churns, heart pounds, breathing quickens, head spins—these are well-known indicators of a panic attack. Whether produced by real or imagined events, high anxiety is as debilitating as it sounds, and the physical ramifications are often long-term and more than just a nuisance. However, there is a way to avoid it.

> *A distant but thunderous noise caught the attention of the flock as they followed the Shepherd along the path. When they realized He was leading them towards the sound, their pace*

92

automatically slackened—fear of the unknown is a powerful emotion. Soon, however, they stopped at the bank of a rough, raging river that was announcing its presence with a deafening roar. The Shepherd moved toward a bridge that appeared to be inadequate for passage over the rough waters. Yet He led them with great confidence, and many moved closer to Him to hear His words of comfort and instruction.

Meanwhile, some sheep began to panic, and in their haste to cross over the threatening river, they pushed several others into the water. Despite the resulting commotion, all but one of the waterlogged sheep could get safely to one shore or the other. As this one terrified sheep was swept down the raging river, struggling to stay afloat, it was too focused on its peril to notice the Shepherd running alongside it on the shore.

When the desperate sheep finally took its eyes off the river, it saw the crook of the Shepherd's staff extended over the water, ready to pull it to safety. However, it was still struggling and thrashing about, making it impossible for the Shepherd to get the hook around it; "Calm down," the Shepherd called out. "Don't panic. Let Me rescue you." As the sheep finally

*heeded this advice, the Shepherd was able
to pull it safely onto the shore; great relief
swept across the exhausted flock.*

It appears that the Shepherd led His flock right into a crisis situation. Or did He? For many sheep, *anxiety*—worry about what may happen—began with a rumble in the distance. It grew to *panic*—sudden unreasoning fear—at the sight of the raging river. And for one poor sheep, it became a full-blown panic attack with its heart pounding and head swimming. From the very beginning, however, the Shepherd never stopped leading and guiding the flock on the path to their destination that day. He was neither anxious nor panicked about the river—it was not a crisis.

Many people feel that they live every moment of every day on the edge of a crisis, and this belief, whether real or imagined, affects how they respond to life's ordinary events. I heard it said in a sermon that it is interesting to observe how a simple *bump* on a leg can actually begin to look more a *lump*, and in no time at all, be imagined as a *stump*.[2] Perhaps we can overcome this tendency to panic with sudden, unreasoning fear by focusing on the behavior of our Shepherd. He is neither anxious nor panicked by our situation, and He will continue to lead and guide us to our destination.

Our Shepherd desires that we ignore the anxiety-producing sounds and sites and, instead, meditate on His written words of comfort. Rather than being known as people who always expect disaster, we can be identified by the description in Psalm 112:6-7: "Those who are righteous will be long remembered. They do not fear bad news; they confidently trust the Lord to care for them."

The sheep swept down the rapid river had a reason for concern, but panic did not serve it well. David could undoubtedly identify with the sheep's dilemma, and he was anxious, if not panicked when he wrote in Psalm 69:1-2, "Save me, O God, for the floodwaters are up to my neck. Deeper and deeper I sink into the mire; I can't find a foothold. I am in deep water, and the floods overwhelm me." During his trouble, David called out to God to save Him. "Rescue me, O God, by your saving power." (v. 29)

Sometimes God must wait for us to get out of the way before He can save us. As this scenario shows, the Shepherd rescued the sheep when it stopped trying to save itself and turned to Him. Today, our Shepherd is calling to us, "Calm down, don't panic, and let Me rescue you."

*****

Our Shepherd is with us! Isolation is described as complete separation of a person suffering from a contagious disease. When we submit to the care of our Shepherd, this definition is somewhat inaccurate. We are never *completely* separated or alone because He is always with us, guiding, protecting, rescuing, and comforting us through every situation. During my isolation, the Shepherd answered my prayer for help and never left my side. He did everything a Good Shepherd is known to do.

Chapter 12

THE LOVE OF GOD

"His miracles are his memorial—This God of Grace, this God of Love." (Psalm 111:4, MSG)

God is Love

The first thing I learned in church as a toddler was that *God is love*. This fact was reiterated Sunday after Sunday, memorized, and my initial introduction to the Creator. Still, after over 65 years of loving Him, this fact holds Him forever in my heart and mind. The knowledge that God is love has carried me through all of life's rough moments, including facing death from the coronavirus. Because of this love, I didn't question my circumstance and chose to trust this love.

God's incredible love has always humbled me. I understand David's question in Psalm 8:3-4, "When I look at the night sky and see the work of your fingers— the moon and the stars you set in place—what are mere mortals that you should think about them, human beings that you should care for them?" If I could be so bold as to answer David, I would say it is because *God is love,* and He just can't help Himself.

Why was God so attentive to me during my severe illness, filling my days with peace, hope, and love? He brought to my mind dozens of scripture verses, even with many medications in my body that affected my thinking. He brought back cherished songs from long ago and filled my mind with new, fresh songs. The Lord was with me when I recalled with gratitude the many miracles and answered prayers throughout my life. His goodness filled me with praise and thanksgiving. Why is He so *mindful of this mere mortal* to spare my life? Because He loves me, and "His miracles are his memorial—This God of Grace, *this God of Love.*" (Psalm 111:4, MSG)

Leaving the Foyer

While enjoying God's presence during my morning devotions several years ago, He impressed this thought to me: *My heart is like an enormous mansion. Most often, my children enter through the front door but never leave the foyer. How unnatural this is.*

Children usually run and romp through their homes, exploring every nook and cranny, and often discover things even unknown to their parents. From the Lord's impression that day, I understood that He is calling His children to intimacy with Him. Our God, filled with more love than He can contain, created us to be the recipients of that great love. We will never answer His call for intimacy without *seeking* to comprehend this love. Of course, we also will never wholly fathom God's love for us, but *intimacy* is the result of seeking it. We need to leave the foyer, open every door, and step through to new dimensions of His love. In doing this, we will never run out of areas for exploration in the vast heart of God.

For many years, singer George Beverly Shea traveled with Dr. Billy Graham to cities worldwide for gospel crusades. He blessed congregations far and wide with his deep rich voice as he sang in each meeting. One of the songs for which he is best known is entitled, "The Love of God." He sang it with such feeling that, even as a young girl, I knew Mr. Shea had experienced God's love in a profound way. The chorus is as follows:

> *Oh, love of God, how rich and pure!*
> *How measureless and strong!*
> *It shall forevermore endure*
> *The saints' and angels' song.*[1]

"The Love of God" was written in 1917 by Frederick M. Lehman, a pastor from the midwestern United States. Impressed by a poem read by an evangelist at a camp meeting one night, Lehman jotted down the words. According to the evangelist, the poem was discovered scratched on a prison wall 200 years earlier. Years later, Pastor Lehman moved to California just as the United States entered World War I. Times were hard, and he worked long hours at a citrus packing house to survive. Stirred by a sermon he heard one Sunday, he sat down amid the packing crates and penned two verses of a hymn about the love of God. Even in this difficult moment in his life, Pastor Lehman chose to focus on the unchanging love of God.

When pondering over the third verse for his hymn, he remembered the poem he had jotted down 50 years earlier at the camp meeting. It fit perfectly! This verse beautifully complements the words that God shared with me years ago regarding the vastness of His love:

> *Could we with ink the ocean fill,*
> *And were the skies of parchment made;*
> *Were ev'ry stalk on earth a quill,*
> *And ev'ry man a scribe by trade;*
> *To write the love of God above*
> *Would drain the ocean dry;*
> *Nor could the scroll contain the whole*
> *Tho' stretched from sky to sky.*[2]

God's love is so vast that we could never exhaust its depths, but shouldn't we try?

The Dimensions of God's Love

"I ask [the Father] that with both feet planted firmly on love, you'll be able to take in with all followers of Jesus the *extravagant dimensions of Christ's love*. Reach out and experience the breadth! Test its length! Plumb the depths! Rise to the heights! Live full lives, full in the fullness of God." (Ephesians 3:17-19, MSG, emphasis added)

In Paul's prayer for the Ephesians, he asked God to strengthen them by His Spirit (verse 16), then prayed that they *take in the extravagant dimensions of Christ's love* and live *in the fullness of God* (verses 17-19, MSG). This prayer may seem like a tall order for God to accomplish in the lives of the newly-converted Ephesians, but as Paul goes on to say in verse 20, "God can do anything you know..." And He can.

Take in the extravagant dimensions of Christ's love. Paul wanted the Ephesians to do more than mentally understand that God loved them. He wanted them to *take in* or comprehend through personal experience the love that God had for them. He went on to encourage them to, "Reach out and experience the breadth! Test its length! Plumb the depths! Rise to the heights!" (3:18) If we unpack verse 18 in the manner described in Chapter 3 and meditate on each component, we *begin* to comprehend something about God's love.

Breadth. Experience it! God's love is for everyone. God's love is colorblind, no exceptions. No one has sinned too much or run from Him too fast to escape His love. David explained in Psalm 139:7,9-10, "Is there any place I can go to avoid your Spirit? to be out of your sight? If I flew on morning's wings to the far western horizon, You'd find me in a minute—you're already there waiting!" (MSG) From east to west, His love encompasses everyone. Experience the breadth of God's love – it's for you.

Length. Test it! God's love has always been, and it always will be. It was present when he formed Adam from the dust of the earth and when He created you and me, "You know me inside and out, you know every bone in my body; You know exactly how I was made, bit by bit, how I was sculpted from nothing into something." (Psalm 139:15, MSG) His love did not end before He created us, and we haven't missed out on it. His love is eternal.

Depth. Dig deep to discover it! "If I go underground, you're there!" (Psalm 139:8, MSG) This generous love of God is deeper than we can plumb, yet so freely given to us. "Have you ever come on anything quite like this extravagant generosity of God, this deep, deep wisdom? It's way over our heads. We'll never figure it out." (Romans 11:33, MSG) But what a joy to dive in and experience all that we can!

Heights. Rise to it! "If I climb to the sky, you're there!" (Psalm 139:7, MSG) Above the fray of those who want to take it from us, God's love is so high that nothing can touch it. We are safe and secure in His love. "I'm absolutely convinced that nothing—nothing living or dead, angelic or demonic, today or tomorrow, high or low, thinkable or unthinkable—absolutely *nothing* can get between us and God's love because of the way that Jesus our Master has embraced us." (Romans 8:38-39, MSG) Feel His embrace today!

I experienced the *dimensions of Christ's love* during my illness and recovery. I haven't made a dent in comprehending the boundless love of God, but I hope I've left the foyer. In our darkest hour, the love of God shines its brightest, and as we have read, His love is for everyone. "Oh, he even sees me in the dark! At night I'm immersed in the light! It's a fact: darkness isn't dark to you; night and day, darkness and light, they're all the same to you." (Psalm 139:11-12, MSG) He lights up our world with His love!

In Closing

In both our deepest trial and our greatest joy, we are never outside of God's abiding love. I don't know what you are walking through today, but I can testify that He is with you. I pray that through reading my story, you have discovered strategies and solutions to guide you along the way.

The *hidden words* memorized from scripture are a continual source of strength and guidance, whether in a sickbed, driving down the road, or encouraging a friend. The Holy Spirit prompts our memories and brings forth what we need at the perfect moment. God's Word never falls short of its intended destination.

Meditate on His Word, take it apart phrase by phrase, word by word. As you pray about its meaning, apply it to your circumstance, and repeat it several times. The Word of God is alive and current to meet every challenge we are facing.

Remember the story I relayed about the old hymn, "I See a Crimson Stream of Blood?" I had lost my focus, and fear was standing at the door. When I turned my attention to the Lord, and away from the challenge I was facing, He provided just what I needed to bring me peace. His *breath from Heaven* changed everything that day. Stay focused on Him!

When sleep alludes us, He gives us *songs in the night* that cause us to *wake the dawn* with a song of praise, filling us with joy. When we start our day focused on Him, the challenges we face are under the watchful care of our Lord.

We need to get our minds off our problem and *get our praise on!* We place our negatives at the foot of the cross and praise Him regardless of how we feel, truly a *sacrifice of praise*. Go back to Chapter 6 and join with David and his long list of praises found in Psalm 145. Our praise will bless Him!

"Faith wins, always in the past, always in the future and always now!" No matter what giant you face today or in the future, focus on the bountiful, *humongous* promises of God rather than on negative reports. Let's make every effort to *amaze* the Lord with our faith like the Roman soldier—show him up! And don't give up! May our persistent faith determine our destiny as we walk in the privileges and authority of our Father. Faith Wins!

A heart of *gratitude* will bless the Lord and all who receive our words of thanks. Remember God's faithfulness, His mighty works throughout your life, with gratitude. Remember His healing touch. Be grateful for the present, regardless of your circumstance, and be thankful for your future because He is already there!

Your earnest *prayers* for others will bring about miracles for them, too. Be certain that your *fervent* prayer is unhindered and offered with a pure heart. Our loved ones and friends deserve nothing less. We can boldly approach His throne with this confidence, "God can do anything, you know—far more than you could ever imagine or guess or request in your wildest dreams!" (Ephesians 3:20, MSG)

Open your heart to the *fresh songs*, the new songs that God is longing to give you. If 12-year-old Giana submitted herself to the Lord in this way, how much more should mature believers be yielded to Him? In your trials, let God's voice sing through you with comfort and encouragement—*It's already won, already won. The victory is mine; I have the plans.*

Have you accepted the Lord as your Savior? When you do, at that moment, He becomes your *Shepherd* to guide you throughout your life along restful waters, through dark valleys until you dwell in His House forever. His rod and staff, through His Word, offer the best guidance available. I can't imagine walking the path of illness I experienced without the Shepherd by my side, often carrying me during my darkest hours. *The Lord is my Shepherd.*

The *dimensions of God's love* are unexplainable yet available to everyone. We will never understand His great love, but He invites us to discover its breadth, its depth, its length, its heights, and experience as much as we can contain. God created us for this purpose—*leave the foyer* and explore!

*****

Do you believe that God will touch you in your trials just as He did for me? Whether a health problem, a broken heart, financial loss, betrayal, or loss of any kind, God has promised to walk with us through to the other side of our trial. Perhaps you feel abandoned by Him because answers have not come quickly. I understand. As I write this book, I am still in recovery, and it has been a recovery hampered by many complications from the coronavirus and the extensive medicines I received. I find myself once again running to the Lord for His help and peace. Another scripture that my dear mom repeated to me regularly throughout my youth is found in Isaiah 30:18, "So the Lord must wait for you to come to him so he can show you his *love and compassion*. For the Lord is a faithful God. Blessed are those who wait for his help." (MSG) *He waits to be more gracious*. Run to Him, focus on His Word, remember His past mercies, and thank Him!

The most amazing miracle healing of my life was the day I walked out of the hospital, a day the medical staff thought might not come. It was Friday, April 10, Good Friday! The stripes my precious Lord bore on the cross reached across the centuries and brought healing to my body. My husband called it, "Best Friday!" And at home, after a 21-day separation, we gave thanks and observed Communion together. Best Friday, indeed!

NOTES

Chapter 2 – Hidden Words
1. Dr. Caroline Leaf, Facebook, April 5, 2016
Available at: www.facebook.com/drleaf
(Assessed: June 14, 2020)

Chapter 3 – Meditation
1. *How to Win Over Depression*
Dr. Tim LaHaye. Zondervan, Published 1974.
2. *Primal. A Quest for the Lost Soul of Christianity*
Mark Batterson. Multnomah Books, Published 2009. Pg. 76
3. Mark Batterson, Facebook, May 8, 2020
Available at: www.facebook.com/MarkBatterson
(Assessed: June 21, 2020)

Chapter 4 - Breath from Heaven
1. Marshall, Garry. *Runaway Bride*. 1999; United States: Paramount Pictures
2. *Switch On Your Brain: The Key to Peak Happiness, Thinking, and Health,* Dr. Caroline Leaf. Baker Books, Published 2013. Pg. 14
3. Ibid.
4. "I see a Crimson Stream of Blood." G.T. Haywood, 1920. Public Domain

Chapter 5 – Songs in the Night
1. "I am Thine, Oh Lord." Fanny Crosby, 1875. Public Domain

Chapter 7 – Faith Wins!
1. "The Solid Rock." Lyrics: Edward Mote, 1834. Music: William Bradbury, 1863. Public Domain

Chapter 10 – Giana's Song
1. "Turn Your Eyes Upon Jesus." Helen Lemmel, 1922. Public Domain
2. The Erwin Brothers. *I Can Only Imagine.* 2018; United States: Lionsgate

Chapter 11 – The Lord is My Shepherd
1. Copied selections: *Intimate Moments with the Shepherd – Guidance Through the Challenges of Life,* Phyllis Benigas Creation House, Published 2008.
2. Notes from a sermon by John Mason, www.freshword.com

Chapter 12 – The Love of God
1. "The Love of God." Frederick M. Lehman, 1917. Public Domain
2. Ibid.

ABOUT THE AUTHOR

Author, speaker, minister, mom, and whatever hat is handed to her, Phyllis Benigas embraces life with a dependence on the Lord for His guidance, His wisdom, and His heartbeat. Her ministry will encourage yet challenge when necessary. And it will draw each one into a deeper, more intimate relationship with God.

The phrase *large Italian family* aptly describes Phyllis' early years at home in Minnesota, growing up with four brothers and two sisters. It was at the tender age of three, at her own request, that Phyllis was introduced to the Lord as she knelt with her mother at a sunny kitchen window and repeated a prayer of repentance. Neither recalls what precipitated her request that day, but following that prayer, she responded, with tears streaming down her face, "I feel so clean inside." Since that early encounter with the Lord, she follows His path with joy, grateful for His grace when her steps falter and for His guidance through difficult moments.

After attending North Central University, Phyllis married Tom Benigas, the love of her life, and has served alongside him for the past 49 years in ministry. They ministered as youth pastors in Minnesota, Colorado, and Florida. Tom and Phyllis directed the Peninsular Florida District of the Assemblies of God Youth Department program, located in Lakeland, Florida, for 24 years. They enjoyed leading youth camps, statewide conventions, youth pastor conferences, outreaches, and youth mission trips, as well as ministering in churches.

Phyllis served on the Assemblies of God World Missions Board for a term and managed A/G missionary itineration in Florida for 22 years. It gave her great joy to assist missionaries in raising funds to return to the field of their calling.

Phyllis and Tom presently work as appointed Assemblies of God missionaries to Europe, serving at Continental Theological Seminary in Brussels, Belgium, where Phyllis assists with the student mentoring and counseling programs. They also work with the Fellowship of European International Churches, traveling extensively to assist international churches with preaching, seminars, and mentoring.

In 2008, she wrote a devotional book entitled, *Intimate Moments with the Shepherd – Guidance through the Challenges of Life,* published by Creation House.

With a personal ministry to women, Phyllis enjoys speaking at women's meetings, retreats, and conferences. She comments, "It is a delight for me to share with women the blessing that comes from stepping past our struggles, insecurities, and heartaches into an understanding of our purpose. Once we discover the fulfillment that comes from a daily intimate relationship with our Creator, our challenges no longer rob us of peace and joy but become the instruments of growth and character-building that God intends."

Phyllis is proud of their two married children and four grandchildren who serve the Lord and minister with fervor.

Contact Phyllis:
phyllisbenigas@gmail.com
phyllisbenigas.com